CHECKING THE BOXES
WRITING UNITS WITH CHECKLISTS

Written and Designed By Karen Langdon

Copyright © 2014 Karen Langdon
All rights reserved by author.
Permission to copy for classroom use only.

ISBN: 978-0-9875308-6-8

This book is dedicated to all young writers. Be brave. Your words can change the world.

"I can shake off everything as I write; my sorrows disappear, my courage is reborn."
~ Anne Frank

"When you don't have anything to do, you can write. You can write about what you like - no one tells you what to write. I think of what I like best, and I think about what they would do with a problem."
~ Hannah, age 9

Table of Contents

- A Guide to Teaching With Checklists ———————————— 2
- Yearlong Pacing Guide ———————————————————— 4
- Personal Narratives Unit ——————————————————— 5
- Small Moments Unit —————————————————————— 15
- Writing For Readers Unit ——————————————————— 25
- Opinion Writing with Letters Unit ——————————————— 35
- "How To" Books Unit ————————————————————— 57
- "How To" Books Mentor Texts ————————————————— 81
- "All About" Books Basic Unit —————————————————— 101
- "All About" Books Advanced Unit ———————————————— 135
- "All About" Books Mentor Texts ————————————————— 171
- Beginning, Middle, & End Mentor Texts —————————————— 213
- Licensing Acknowledgements —————————————————— 259
- Contacts and Terms of Use —————————————————— 263

Please note: Many pages in this book do not have page numbers on them. This is because they are designed for you to copy and use with your students. Page numbers are only included on information pages to help guide you through the book.

A Guide to Teaching With Checklists

These writing units were developed to provide concrete structures to help students improve the craft and quality of their writing in a developmentally appropriate way.

Young writers - only five and six years old! - will begin to write *and* revise, give useful and constructive feedback to peers, and include powerful and effective details in their writing. I hope you find this method to be as impactful as I have!

The pacing guide for each unit will provide you with step by step instructions on how to incorporate the checklists into your teaching. The main concept is that young children need concrete feedback on what to do. The checklists provide them with visual reminders, every time they write, on what they need to include in their work. They are self managed rubrics that students use every day - even multiple times a day!

This type of teaching begins with an immersion phase, where you and your students spend time together exploring books in the chosen genre. You will encourage them to notice certain features that characterize the genre. When you later introduce the checklist, students are primed to tell you what they think the important features are! This gives them ownership over the genre. Regardless of what your students come up with, you can artfully use their words to co-create a checklist (one which you already have prepared!)

After checklists and checklist paper become a part of the room, your job is to guide students to refer to them often. When you confer with students, you should ask them to tell you what parts of the checklist they still need to include. You can help them evaluate their own work. This also gives you an easy suggestion for conferring, even for very strong writers - you can always turn to the checklist to give them concrete feedback on how to improve their work.

Young children often struggle with partner work, and they need to be taught the words to use when talking to peers about their writing. When you use checklists during a daily share time, you are giving ALL students a job (they should be listening for the components of the checklist while a peer shares their piece), and you are helping them to develop constructive feedback. They can learn to say, "I noticed you included the who and what and setting, but I don't know how you are feeling in the piece. Maybe you can add that tomorrow." The advisors learn to listen and read with intent, and the writers learn to revise.

Finally, checklists offer an excellent method for extending the time students spend on a piece. Rather than rushing through one line pieces, or finishing every piece with, "and it was fun," they now have real concepts of how to write quality work.

Each unit in this book has a specifically designed checklist to highlight key features of the genre. You should only be using ONE checklist in the classroom at a given time. There is one exception to this. Once you have taught the "Writing for Readers" unit, this checklist can remain up in the classroom as a reminder that these features are important in every genre. Otherwise, remove a checklist from the room as you conclude a unit, and move on to a new one.

Once you begin teaching writing with checklists, you will never want to turn back! Enjoy!

Karen Langdon

Year Long Pacing Guide

Unit 1 Launching Writing Workshop	Unit 2 Personal Narratives	Unit 3 Small Moments
Establish routines and expectations. Encourage children to develop stories and record them on paper. About 6 weeks	Children write true stories about their own experiences. Follow pacing guide included. About 6 weeks	Children "zoom in on intersting parts of their narratives and add sensory details. Follow pacing guide included. About 6 weeks
Unit 4 Writing For Readers	Unit 5 Opinion Writing - Letters	Unit 6 "How To" Books
Children attend to conventions to make their writing readable. Follow pacing guide included. About 5 - 6 weeks	Children write letters expressing opions and support their opinions with evidence. Follow pacing guide included. About 5 - 6 weeks	Children write procedural texts to teach readers how to do something. Follow pacing guide included. About 6 weeks
Unit 7 ""All About" Books	Special Note about "All About" Units	Optional End of the Year Work
Children research and write informational texts about a topic. Follow pacing guide included. About 6 weeks	Included are two "All About" books units. One is basic and one is advanced. Choose the unit to best suit your students' needs, or use both in order to differentiate for different students.	Beginning, Middle, and End This resource can be used any time throughout the year, but works well along side the Small Moments unit. Variable duration.

Who / What

Setting

Feeling

PERSONAL NARRATIVES

Pacing Guide

Lesson/Activity Description	Time
Immersion: Read and expose students to many examples of personal narratives. Reread one or two texts repeatedly that will be primary mentor texts. This should take place while you are wrapping up the previous unit (publishing, celebrating, etc.) It will happen during your read aloud portion of the day, not writing workshop.	One Week
Close Study: Explain that the students will now listen to their main mentor text again, this time as writers. Ask them to pay attention to the words that the author chose to use. You will want to delicately call their attention to certain things. For example, they will need to notice that there is a narrator that uses the words I, me, and my. You will want to discuss the setting, and point out that authors write about things that are important to them, and that they feel strongly about. Have the students compile a list of features they noticed in the personal narrative mentor text/s.	2-3 Days
Checklist Introduction: Show the children that you used the discussion you had as a class to develop a checklist for personal narratives. Explain that every personal narrative needs to have several features: it needs to be about somebody (usually yourself) doing something (who/what). There needs to be a setting, and in good personal narratives, we know how the narrator is feeling. Demonstrate writing a piece using the checklist.	1 Day
Minilessons: Spend the next several weeks teaching minilessons as needed. You will be doing many lessons on stretching out words, but be sure to return to the features of the genre regularly. Use the checklist daily during share time.	3 - 4 Weeks
Peer Revision: Have students select a piece that they would like to publish. Then have them work with a partner, using the peer checklist, to revise their work.	1 Day
Publishing: Have students revise their chosen piece, using the feedback from their writing partners. They can then come to you for feedback. (Begin immersion in next unit).	3 Days
Celebration: Share the published pieces with an audience and celebrate!	1 Day

Name _____   Date _____

| Who/What | Setting | Feeling |

Name _____   Date _____

| Who/What | Setting | Feeling |

Written By: _____

Date: _____

| Who/What ☐ | Setting ☐ | Feeling ☐ |

Written By: _____

Date: _____

| Who/What ☐ | Setting ☐ | Feeling ☐ |

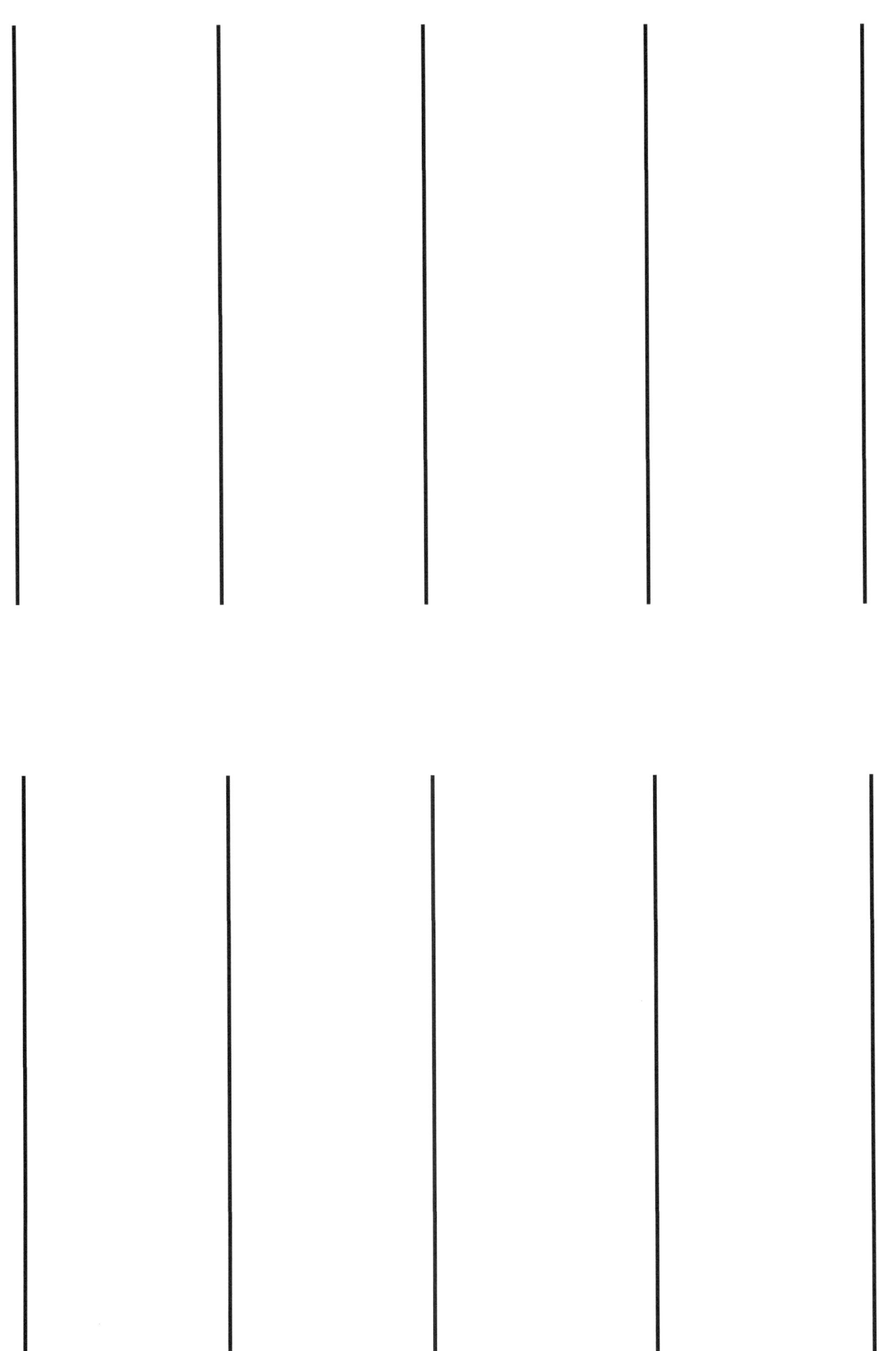

Author: _____ Peer Advisor: _____

Who/What ☐

Setting ☐

Feeling ☐

Author: _____ Peer Advisor: _____

Who/What ☐

Setting ☐

Feeling ☐

Who/What

Setting

Feeling

 Who / What

 Setting

 Feeling / Five Senses

 Beginning, Middle, End

SMALL MOMENTS

Pacing Guide

Lesson/Activity Description	Time
Immersion: Read and expose students to many examples of personal narratives that include small moments. Begin to use the term "small moments." Reread one or two texts repeatedly that will be primary mentor texts. This should take place while you are wrapping up the previous unit (publishing, celebrating, etc.) It will take place during your read aloud portion of the day, not writing workshop.	One Week
Close Study: Explain that the students will now listen to their main mentor text again, this time as writers. Ask them to notice all the small moments in the text. Compile a list as a group of all of the small moments in the text. Demonstrate how the book itself is a big story, but you can zoom in on special parts, or moments. Model "zooming in" on your favorite moment in the book, and draw/write about that moment. Then have students zoom in on their favorite moments, writing and drawing about them. Compile a class book of your favorite small moments from the mentor text.	2-3 Days
Checklist Introduction: Explain that small moments are a version of personal narratives, and you will be using a similar checklist. Explain that they will now make their writing better by using sensory language, and ensuring a detailed beginning, middle, and end. Demonstrate using the checklist.	1 Day
Minilessons: Spend the next several weeks teaching minilessons as needed. You will need to teach how to use sensory language, how to write a quality beginning, middle, and end, and how to use the checklist to revise. Include any others lessons as needed. Use the checklist daily during share time.	3 - 4 Weeks
Peer Revision: Have students select a piece that they would like to publish. Then have them work with a partner, using the peer checklist, to revise their work.	1 Day
Publishing: Have students revise their chosen piece, using the feedback from their writing partners. They can then come to you for feedback. (Begin immersion in next unit).	3 Days
Celebration: Share the published pieces with an audience and celebrate!	1 Day

Name _____   Date _____

| Who/What | Setting | Feeling / Five Senses | Beginning, Middle, End |

Name _____   Date _____

| Who/What | Setting | Feeling / Five Senses | Beginning, Middle, End |

Written By: _____

Date: _____

Who/What	Setting
Feeling / Five Senses	Beginning, Middle, End

Written By: _____

Date: _____

Who/What	Setting
Feeling / Five Senses	Beginning, Middle, End

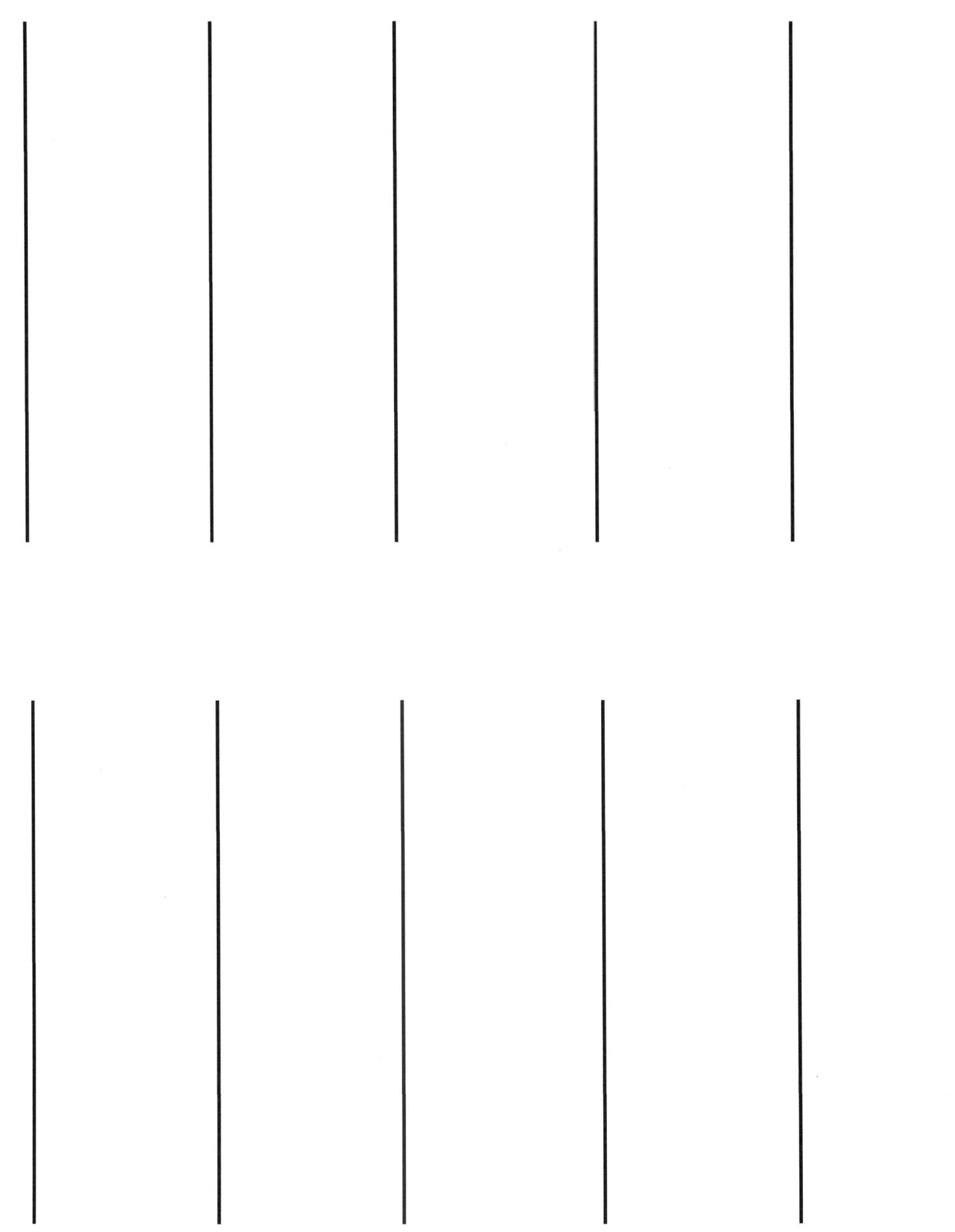

Author: _____ Peer Advisor: _____

 Who/What ☐

 Setting ☐

 Feeling/Five Senses ☐

 Beginning, Middle, End ☐

Author: _____ Peer Advisor: _____

 Who/What ☐

 Setting ☐

 Feeling/Five Senses ☐

 Beginning, Middle, End ☐

Who/What

Setting

Feeling/Five Senses

Beginning, Middle, End

Spaces Between Words

Punctuation

Lowercase Letters

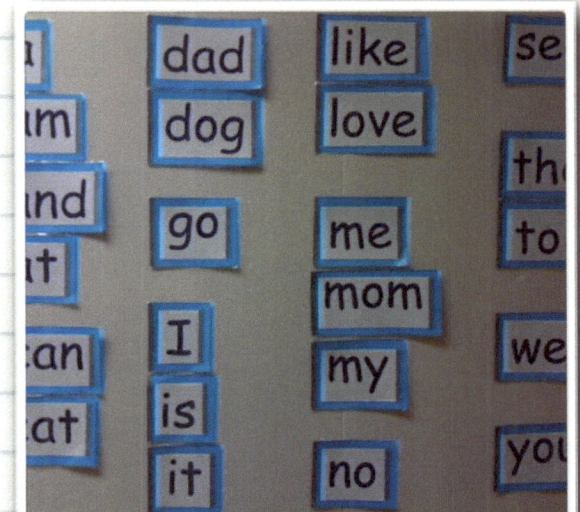

Word Wall Words

WRITING FOR READERS

Pacing Guide

Lesson/Activity Description	Time
Immersion: This should be started while you are wrapping up the previous unit (publishing, celebrating, etc.) It will take place during your read aloud portion of the day, not during writing workshop. Read and expose students to many examples of your chosen genre. Because this unit focuses on writing conventions, you can allow students to write in any genre - narrative, informational, fantasy, pattern books, etc.	3 Days
Close Study: Explain to students that their writing is going to begin to look more like it does in books. Using mentor texts in your chosen genre, show the students how there are spaces between words, lowercase letters (except for specific reasons), punctuation, and word wall words spelled correctly.	1 Day
Checklist Introduction: Show the children how you used the discussion that you had as a class to develop a checklist for writers (in every genre!) Explain that all writing needs to be readable. Focus on the features of the checklist (spaces between words, lowercase letters, punctuation, and word wall words) as ways they can make their writing easier to read. Demonstrate writing a piece using the checklist.	1 Day
Minilessons: Spend the next several weeks teaching minilessons as needed. You will be doing many lessons focusing on these conventions. Have students practice fixing up examples that *you* write, examples written by other students, and their own work. Use the checklist daily during share time.	3 - 4 Weeks
Peer Revision: Have students select a piece that they would like to publish. Have them work with a partner, using the peer checklist, to edit their work.	1 Day
Publishing: Have students edit their chosen piece, using the feedback from their writing partners. They can then come to you for feedback. (Begin immersion in next unit).	3 Days
Celebration: Share the published pieces with an audience and celebrate! This checklist now becomes an *additional* checklist for all writing to follow.	1 Day

Name _____   Date _____

| Spaces Between Words | Punctuation | Lowercase Letters | Word Wall Words |

Name _____   Date _____

| Spaces Between Words | Punctuation | Lowercase Letters | Word Wall Words |

Written By: _____

Date: _____

Spaces Between Words	Punctuation	Lowercase Letters	Word Wall Words

Written By: _____

Date: _____

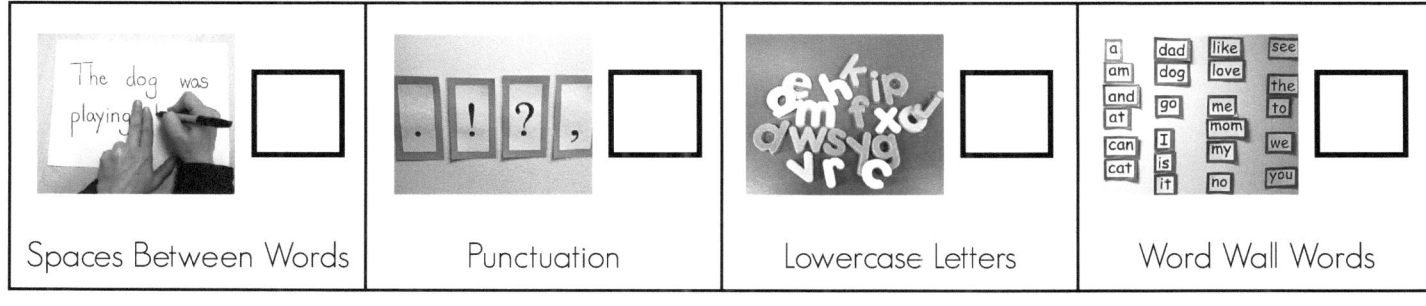

| Spaces Between Words | Punctuation | Lowercase Letters | Word Wall Words |

Author: _____ Peer Advisor: _____

Spaces Between Words

☐

Lowercase Letters

☐

Punctuation

☐

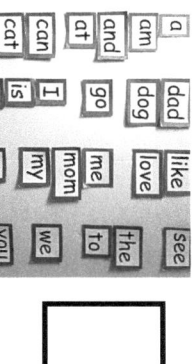

Word Wall Words

☐

Author: _____ Peer Advisor: _____

Spaces Between Words

☐

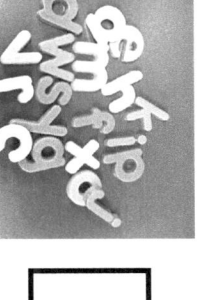

Lowercase Letters

☐

Punctuation

☐

Word Wall Words

☐

Spaces Between Words

Lowercase Letters

Punctuation

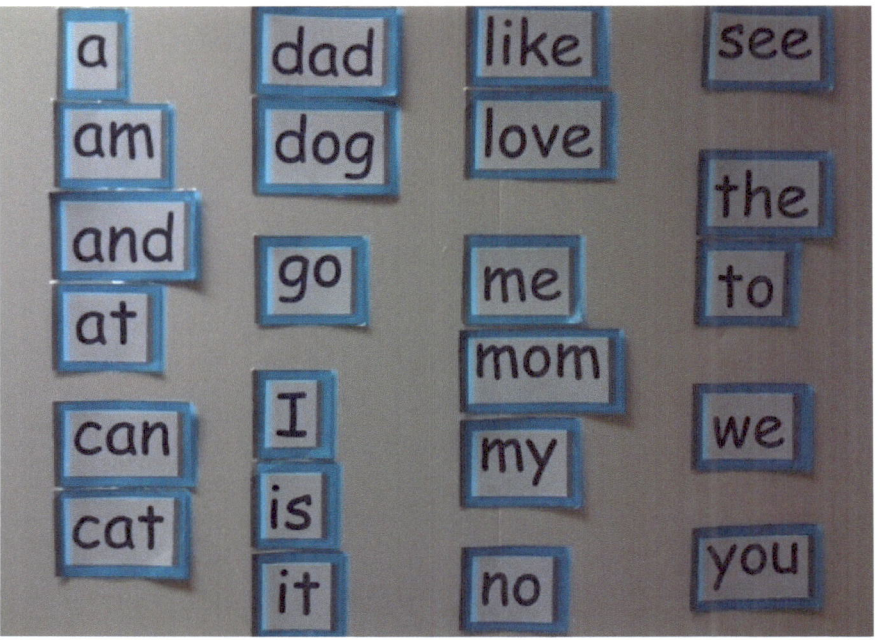

Word Wall Words

"It's not my favorite thing to do, but I am still pretty good at it. I get my ideas from what we did on the weekends and vacations."
~ Brady, age 8

OPINION WRITING
LETTERS

Pacing Guide

Lesson/Activity Description	Time
Immersion: This should take place while you are wrapping up the previous unit (publishing, celebrating, etc.) It will take place during your read aloud portion of the day, not writing workshop. Read and expose students to many examples of letters and opinion letters. Because this unit focuses on letters, you may have been immersing them all year. Your morning message, thank you letters, and letters to Santa are all examples! Make sure to read a variety of mentor texts - child written letters, letters in books, teacher written samples, and some that do (and do not) contain opinions.	3 Days Minimum (remember, with this unit, immersion may have been taking place all year!)
Close Study of Letters: Explain to students that they are now going to study letters as writers. Using mentor texts discuss the structure of letters with students.	1 Day
Minilessons: The first group of minilessons should focus on letter writing. Your lessons will cover the structure and purpose of letters. This should be a brief round of lessons.	3 Days
Close Study of Opinion Letters: You will now focus your study in on opinion letters. This should specifically cover how a letter can have an opinion, and is backed by a reason and evidence. Demonstrate writing an opinion letter, and model how to come up with an opinion (possibly about a favorite book), and back up it with evidence.	2 Days
Checklist Introduction: Show the children that you used the discussion you had as a class to develop a checklist for writers that are writing opinion letters. Explain that all opinion writing should have an opinion, a reason, and evidence. Remind them that letters all have a greeting, body, and closing. Model writing a piece and using the checklist.	1 Day
Minilessons: Spend the next several weeks teaching minilessons as needed. You will be doing many lessons focusing on writing opinions and backing them with evidence. Depending on your students, you may include work on different kinds of evidence (text to self or book evidence). Use the checklist daily during share time.	2 - 3 Weeks

Pacing Guide

Lesson/Activity Description	Time
Peer Revision: Have students select a piece that they would like to publish. Then have them work with a partner, using the peer checklist, to revise their work.	1 Day
Publishing: Have students revise and edit their chosen piece, using the feedback from their writing partners. They can then come to you for feedback. (Begin immersion in next unit).	3 Days
Celebration: Share the published pieces with an audience and celebrate!	1 Day

Dear Mrs. Brown,

    My favorite book to read aloud is called <u>The Hello Goodbye Window</u>. It is all about a little girl who is spending the night at her Nana and Poppy's house, and she tells all about the adventures they have. I like the book because it is funny. I especially like the part when she says there is a tiger in the back of the garden, but we can tell it is just a cat. This book is also special to me because it reminds me of visits to my grandparents' house when I was little. We used to work in the garden together too! I hope you enjoy this book!

                                         Sincerely,
                                         Mrs. Daniels

Dear Mrs. Brown,

My favorite book to read aloud is called <u>The Hello Goodbye Window</u>. It is all about a little girl who is spending the night at her Nana and Poppy's house, and she tells all about the adventures they have. I like the book because it is funny. I especially like the part when she says there is a tiger in the back of the garden, but we can tell it is just a cat. This book is also special to me because it reminds me of visits to my grandparents' house when I was little. We used to work in the garden together too! I hope you enjoy this book!

Sincerely,
Mrs. Daniels

Dear Mrs. Brown,

My favorite book to read aloud is called <u>The Hello Goodbye Window</u>. It is all about a little girl who is spending the night at her Nana and Poppy's house, and she tells all about the adventures they have. I like the book because it is funny. I especially like the part when she says there is a tiger in the back of the garden, but we can tell it is just a cat. This book is also special to me because it reminds me of visits to my grandparents' house when I was little. We used to work in the garden together too! I hope you enjoy this book!

                                            Sincerely,
                                            Mrs. Daniels

Dear Mrs. Brown,

    My favorite book to read aloud is called <u>The Hello Goodbye Window.</u> It is all about a little girl who is spending the night at her Nana and Poppy's house, and she tells all about the adventures they have. ==I like the book because it is funny.== I especially like the part when she says there is a tiger in the back of the garden, but we can tell it is just a cat. ==This book is also special to me because it reminds me of visits to my grandparents' house when I was little.== We used to work in the garden together too! I hope you enjoy this book!

                                        Sincerely,
                                        Mrs. Daniels

Dear Mrs. Brown,

    My favorite book to read aloud is called <u>The Hello Goodbye Window.</u> It is all about a little girl who is spending the night at her Nana and Poppy's house, and she tells all about the adventures they have. I like the book because it is funny. I especially like the part when she says there is a tiger in the back of the garden, but we can tell it is just a cat. This book is also special to me because it reminds me of visits to my grandparents' house when I was little. We used to work in the garden together too! I hope you enjoy this book!

                                            Sincerely,
                                            Mrs. Daniels

Greeting, Body, Closing | Opinion | Reason | Evidence

| Greeting, Body, Closing | Opinion | Reason | Evidence |

Greeting, Body, Closing | Opinion | Reason | Evidence

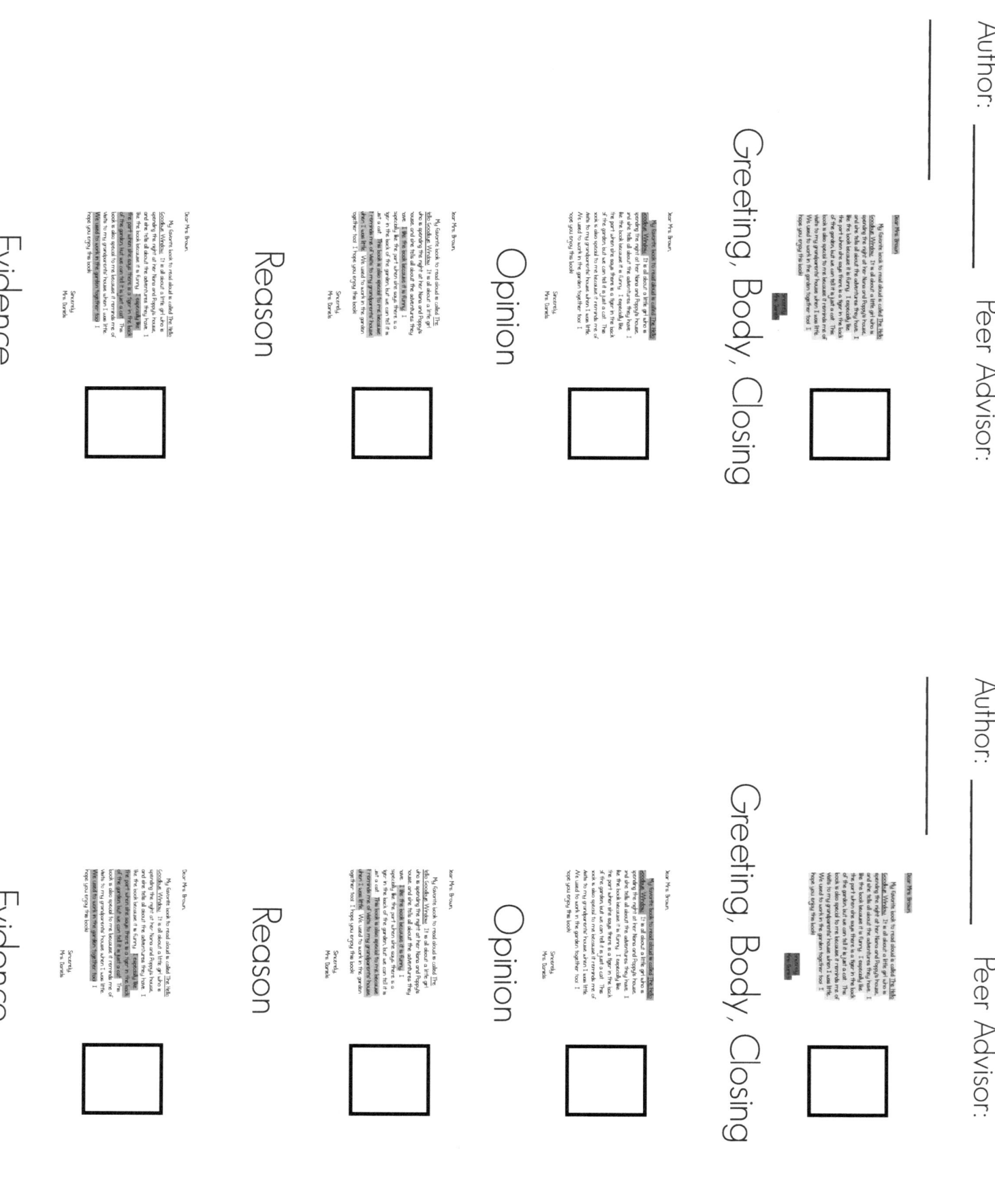

Dear Mrs. Brown,

   My favorite book to read aloud is called The Hello Goodbye Window. It is all about a little girl who is spending the night at her Nana and Poppy's house, and she tells all about the adventures they have. I like the book because it is funny. I especially like the part when she says there is a tiger in the back of the garden, but we can tell it is just a cat. This book is also special to me because it reminds me of visits to my grandparents' house when I was little. We used to work in the garden together too! I hope you enjoy this book!

                            Sincerely,
                            Mrs. Daniels

Greeting, Body, Closing

Dear Mrs. Brown,

   My favorite book to read aloud is called The Hello Goodbye Window. It is all about a little girl who is spending the night at her Nana and Poppy's house, and she tells all about the adventures they have. I like the book because it is funny. I especially like the part when she says there is a tiger in the back of the garden, but we can tell it is just a cat. This book is also special to me because it reminds me of visits to my grandparents' house when I was little. We used to work in the garden together too! I hope you enjoy this book!

                            Sincerely,
                            Mrs. Daniels

Opinion

Dear Mrs. Brown,

My favorite book to read aloud is called The Hello Goodbye Window. It is all about a little girl who is spending the night at her Nana and Poppy's house, and she tells all about the adventures they have. ==I like the book because it is funny.== I especially like the part when she says there is a tiger in the back of the garden, but we can tell it is just a cat. ==This book is also special to me because it reminds me of visits to my grandparents' house when I was little.== We used to work in the garden together too! I hope you enjoy this book!

Sincerely,
Mrs. Daniels

Reason

Dear Mrs. Brown,

My favorite book to read aloud is called The Hello Goodbye Window. It is all about a little girl who is spending the night at her Nana and Poppy's house, and she tells all about the adventures they have. I like the book because it is funny. ==I especially like the part when she says there is a tiger in the back of the garden, but we can tell it is just a cat.== This book is also special to me because it reminds me of visits to my grandparents' house when I was little. ==We used to work in the garden together too!== I hope you enjoy this book!

Sincerely,
Mrs. Daniels

Evidence

Dear Mrs. Johnson,

    I wanted to thank you for all of the work you do in our class. You are such a great help to all of us. We appreciate you!

                              Sincerely,
                              Mrs. Daniels

Dear Dr. Anderson,

   Thank you for presenting to our class about dental health. We learned so much, and you were very funny as well. Thank you for the new tooth brush! We hope you will come back next year.

   Sincerely,
   Mrs. Daniels

Dear Sweetheart,

    I want to tell you about a new book that I read that I think you will love! It is called <u>Silver Seeds</u>. It is a poetry book, and it has poems about all sorts of things that you find in nature. There is one poem about the stars that is especially beautiful. I know how much you love to look at things outside, so I think you will like this book a lot. I can't wait to read it with you!

                                    Love,
                                      Mommy

Dear Mr. Smith,

    I think that we should be able to buy popcorn at school every day. It is a great way to raise money for the school, and it is really yummy.

                                Sincerely,
                                Mrs. Daniels

Dear Mr. Peterson,

    I think that we need some more choices for school lunches. We have pizza too often, and the students get tired of eating the same thing so regularly. I also think that we should have more options so the children can try new things and expand their eating horizons. I hope you consider my request.

                              Sincerely,
                              Mrs. Daniels

Dear Sweetheart,

    I think that you should sleep in your own big boy bed every night. You sleep better when you have more room to stretch out. Your dad and I sleep better when we are not worried about waking you up. You have more room to have your stuffed animals sleep with you when you sleep in your own bed. Finally, you are so proud of yourself when you sleep in your big boy bed! Please consider trying to sleep in your own bed more often.

                                Hugs and kisses,
                                Mommy

Dear Neighbor,

    I think that you should lower the volume on your television when you watch programs late at night. Your volume is up so high that we can hear you downstairs! Sometimes it even wakes my daughter up. It could also be bad for your hearing to have the volume up so high. Please turn it down.

                                    Respectfully,
                                    Your Neighbor

"I think that writing is fun because I can be creative, and I can say whatever I want.."

~ Morgan, age 9

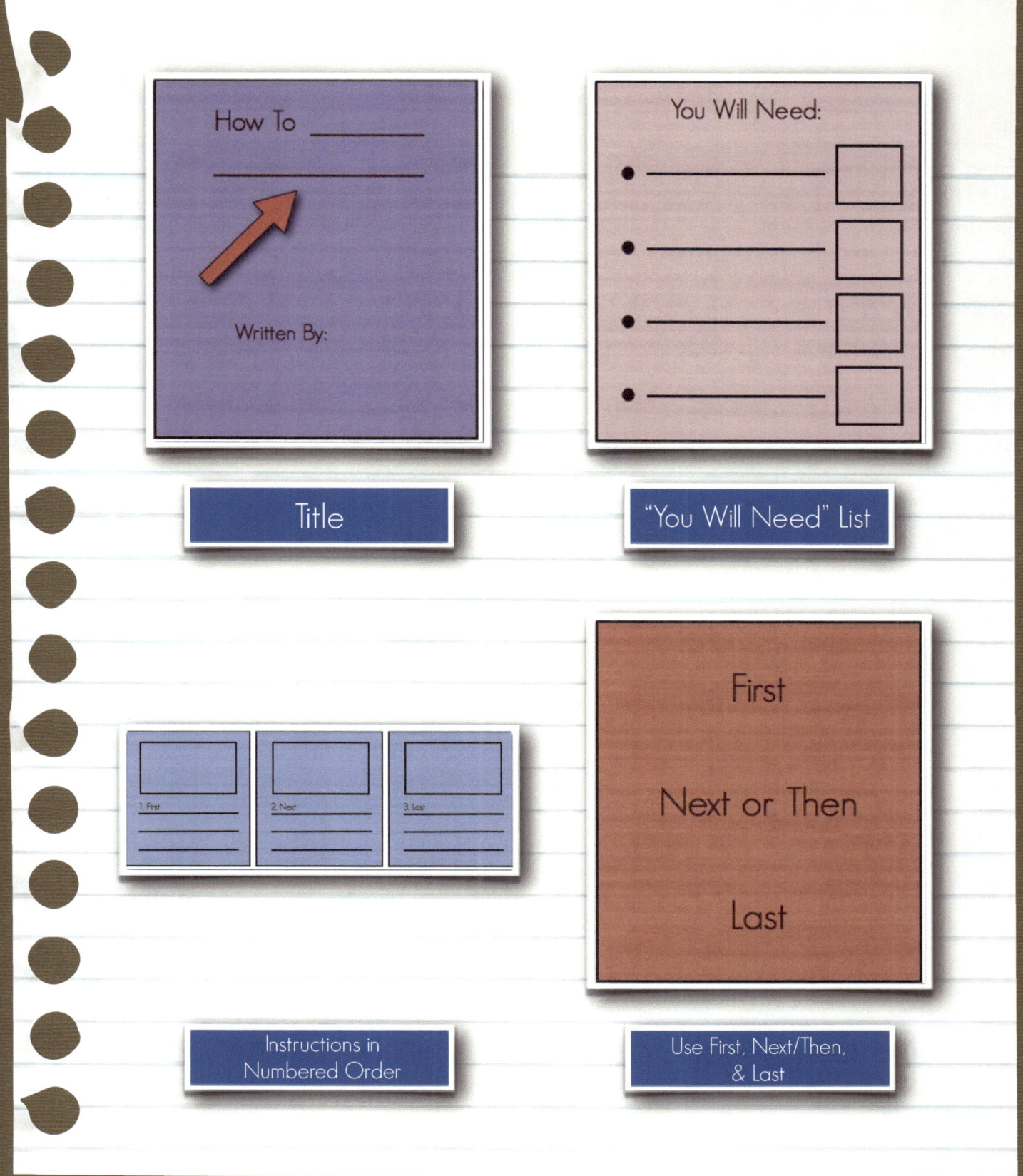

Pacing Guide

Lesson/Activity Description	Time
Immersion Phase 1: This phase is slightly different than with other units. It should begin with general exploring and reading of How To books. This should be just enough to wet the kids' appetite to learn more. I usually start by reading the titles of a huge collection of "how to" books I have brought into the room. Then each day we look at one book a little more carefully. In this way, the kids are eager for me to get to some of the titles I read aloud. The books we read/look at are the ones I plan to use for immersion phase 2. All of the books are available for the kids to look at during reading and choice times.	3-5 Days
Immersion Phase 2: Explain to students that they are now going to *experience* "how to" books. They should keep in mind that they are to be thinking as writers, and to notice what the writers did well, or could have improved. Each day choose one how to lesson, and actually follow the instructions and learn how to do something new. In my room we have learned how to make wrapping paper, hula dance, do origami, do card tricks, do science experiments, make recipes, and make balloon animals. The motivation is through the roof during this phase, and the kids cannot wait to start writing their own how to books. I encourage you to try a variety of activities, and to not shy away from challenging options. If things do not go well, you can have a great discussion about how the writer could have improved the instructions! This work takes the place of my *typical* writing time during this week only.	5 Days
Close Study: Choose your favorite "how to" book example from those that you worked with in the previous week - this example should be a good example of what you want the kids to do. Take a closer look again at the text features, noticing what good "how to" books have.	1 Day
Checklist Introduction: Show the children that you used the discussion you had as a class to develop a checklist for writers that are writing "how to" books. Explain that all "how to" books should have a title, "you will need" list, instructions in numbered order, and transition words such as "first," "next," "then," and "last."	1 Day

Pacing Guide

Lesson/Activity Description	Time
How to Write a How To Book: Explain to the kids that they will soon begin writing their own "how to" books. Show them the "How to make a how to book" poster to explain the process.	½ Day
Expert Lists Part 1: Step 1 in writing a "how to" book is to make a list of things you are an expert at. Demonstrate this as a large group. Compile a class list of things that all of the kids in the class are experts at. Classroom procedures are great for this. Some ideas include: how to go through the lunch line, how to put on snow clothes and get ready to go outside, how to check out a book from the school library, and how to go down a slide. This list should highlight procedures that would ultimately make good how to books, which all the kids can relate to. This is a good time to discourage ideas like "how to say the ABCs" and "how to be nice" because they are difficult to explain.	1 Day
Group Written How To Book: I recommend writing the first "how to" book together as a class. Take your students through the 7 step process, using one of the ideas you came up with on your expert list. I do this as my writing time each day for a few days. Sometimes the kids share the pen, and sometimes I write, but they are involved in developing and sequencing all of the instructions. I use a large, laminated book for this, which I can then reuse. I included photos in this packet. You could also use a paper book, or overhead slides. Once the book is written, invite a guest (another teacher, custodian, etc) in, and see if they can follow the directions successfully. This is a great motivator for the kids to be specific, careful writers!	2-3 Days
Expert Lists Part 2: Now it is finally time to let the kids start the writing process on their own! Spend one day entirely devoted to developing individual expert lists. Before sending them off, I like to feed their ideas a little, to let them know that a wide variety of ideas are acceptable. I might say, "I know _____ is an expert at making snowflakes, _____ is an expert at playing SuperMario Brothers, and _____ is an expert at making fancy bows that match her clothes." This tends to fuel the motivation some more! Have the kids write their own expert list, which will remain in their folder for the whole unit.	1 Day

Pacing Guide

Lesson/Activity Description	Time
Minilessons: The next portion of the unit will involve student work and minilessons as needed. I often find the need to reteach the "you will need" list concept as a minilesson, as kids tend to want to write sentences here, rather than a list. We also often need to discuss the purpose of the list. "The step by step instructions should not tell me to *get* a certain item, because I already got it (by reading the "you will need" list.) The instructions should tell me what to do with it." I start every day with a quick review of the How To poster, as students will be moving through the steps at their own pace. One student might be revising their second book while another student is doing the "you will need" list of their first. As long as they know the steps, this is fine! This is a time when you could use the blank page mentor text to have the kids help you write (the washing hands book on page 37), or you could use this text for a small group of kids who need extra support.	2 Weeks
Peer Revision: Have students select a piece that they would like to publish. Then have them work with a partner, using the peer checklist, to revise and edit their work.	1 Day
Publishing: Have students revise and edit their chosen piece, using the feedback from their writing partners. They can then come to you for feedback. (Begin immersion in next unit).	1-3 Days
Celebration: Share the published pieces with an audience and celebrate!	1 Day

A Note About Mentor Texts: In this unit, having a large selection of mentor texts is critical. I have found that libraries are jammed with great "how to" mentor texts, but "How To" is not always in the title. You might find things like <u>Taking Care of Your Pet Hamster,</u> <u>Being a Snowboarding Star,</u> or <u>Creepy Halloween Crafts.</u> These are all "how to" books. Cookbooks are also excellent "how to" books. Not all of these examples will fulfill the checklist perfectly, and that is fine. Just be sure that the texts you choose for the close study *do* have all of the features you are looking for, and it will be great! Have fun selecting texts, especially with your students' interests in mind!

Anchor Tools

How To Write A "How To" Book Poster Example
(use pages 8-14 to build your own)

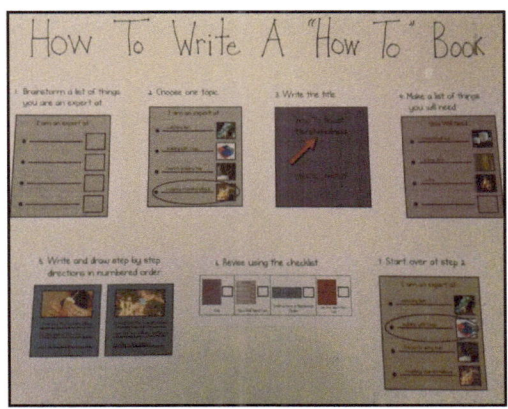

Large Group Wipe Off How To Book
(for group written how to book)

Sample of Finished Booklet
(just copy, cut and staple!)

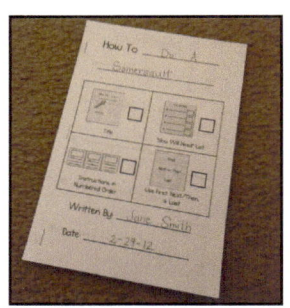

1. Brainstorm a list of things you are an expert at.

2. Choose one topic.

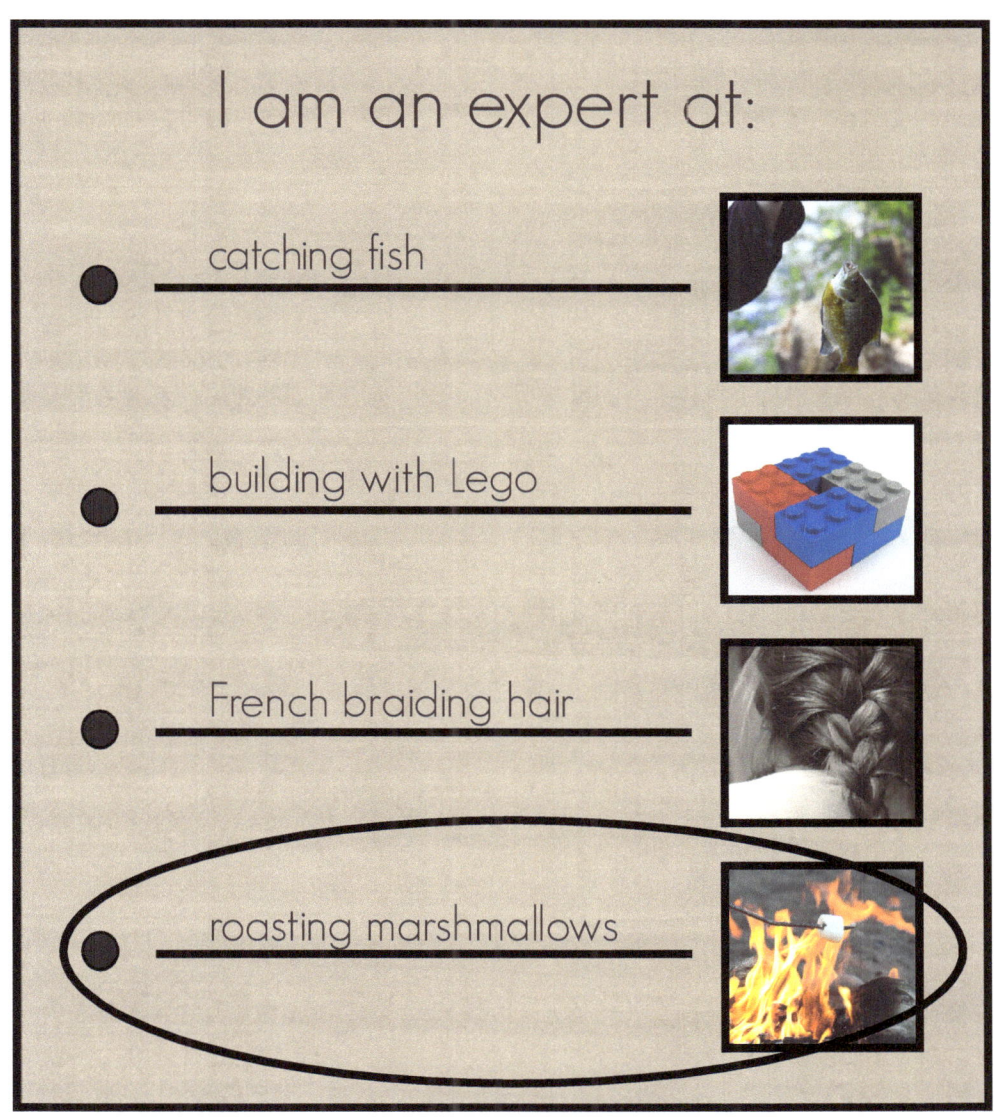

3. Write the title.

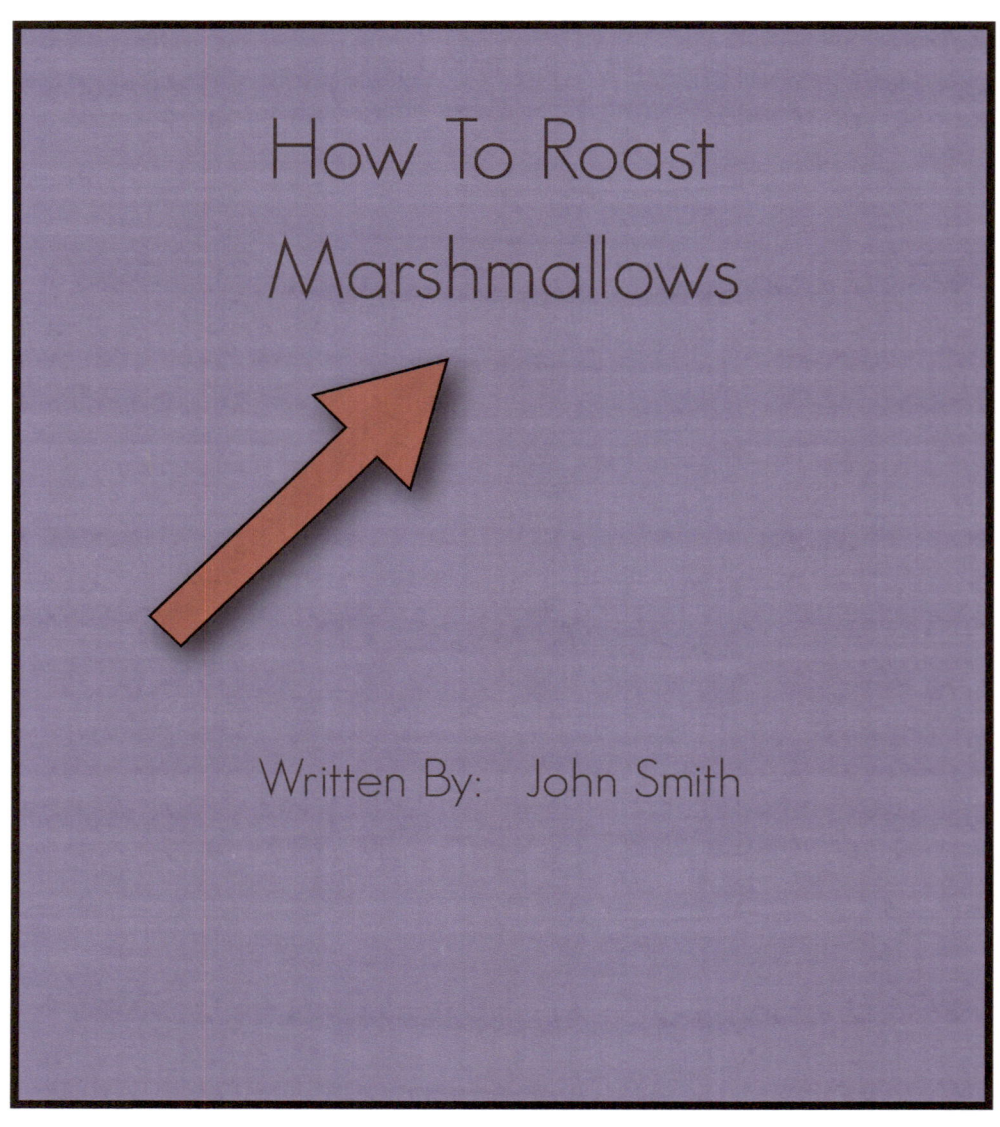

4. Make a list of things you will need.

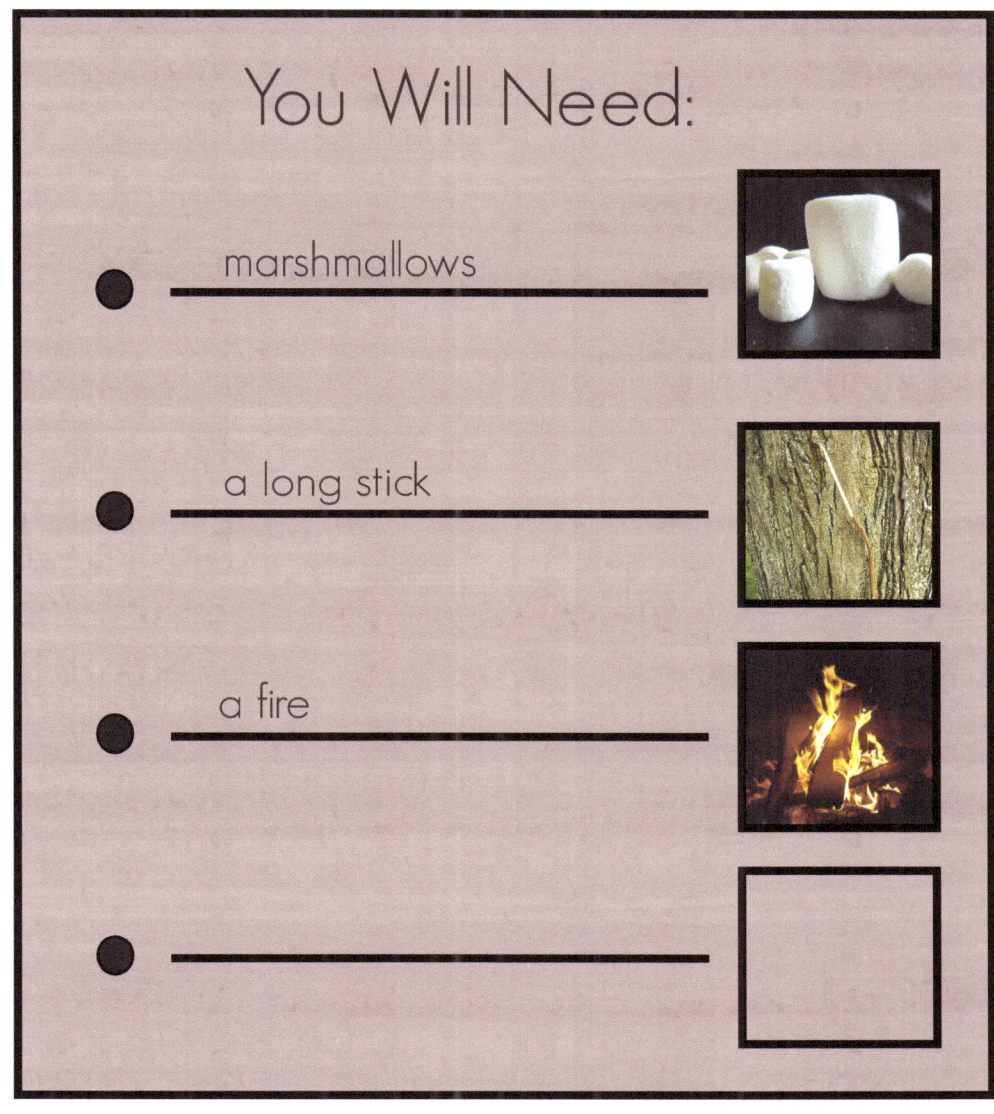

You Will Need:

- marshmallows
- a long stick
- a fire
- _____

5. Write and draw step by step directions in numbered order.

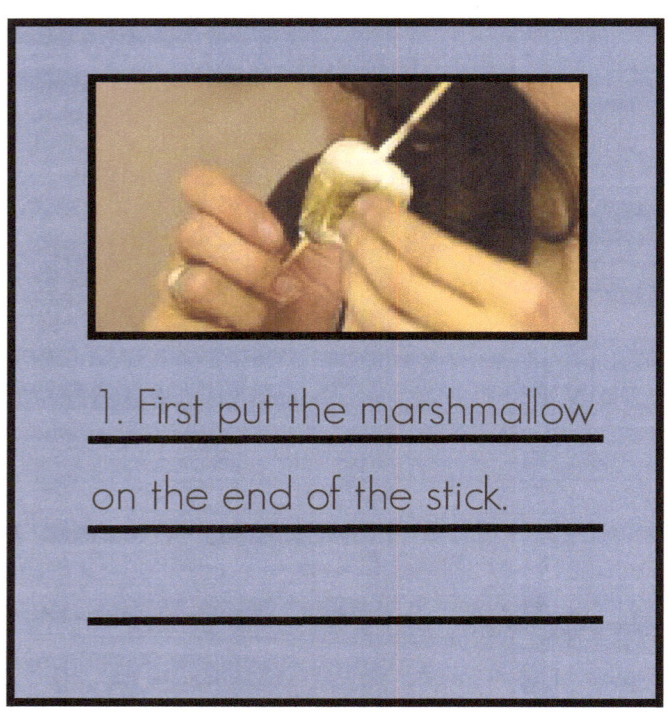

1. First put the marshmallow on the end of the stick.

2. Next hold the marshmallow over the fire without putting it directly in the flames.

6. Revise using the checklist.

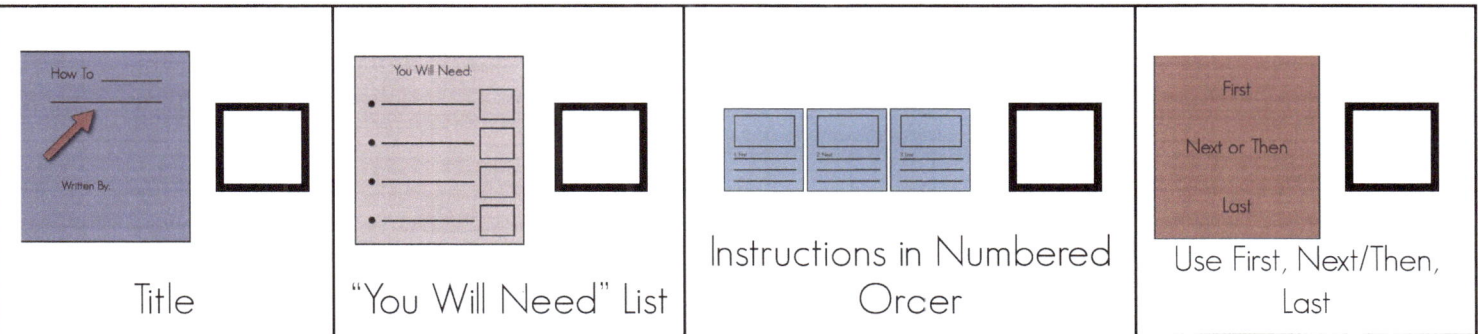

7. Start over at step 2.

Name _____

I am an expert at:

- _____
- _____
- _____
- _____
- _____

How To _____

Title — How To _____ / Written By:

"You Will Need" List

Instructions in Numbered Order

Use First, Next/Then, & Last — First / Next or Then / Last

Written By: _____

Date: _____

How To _____

Title — How To _____ / Written By:

"You Will Need" List

Instructions in Numbered Order

Use First, Next/Then, & Last — First / Next or Then / Last

Written By: _____

Date: _____

You Will Need:

You Will Need:

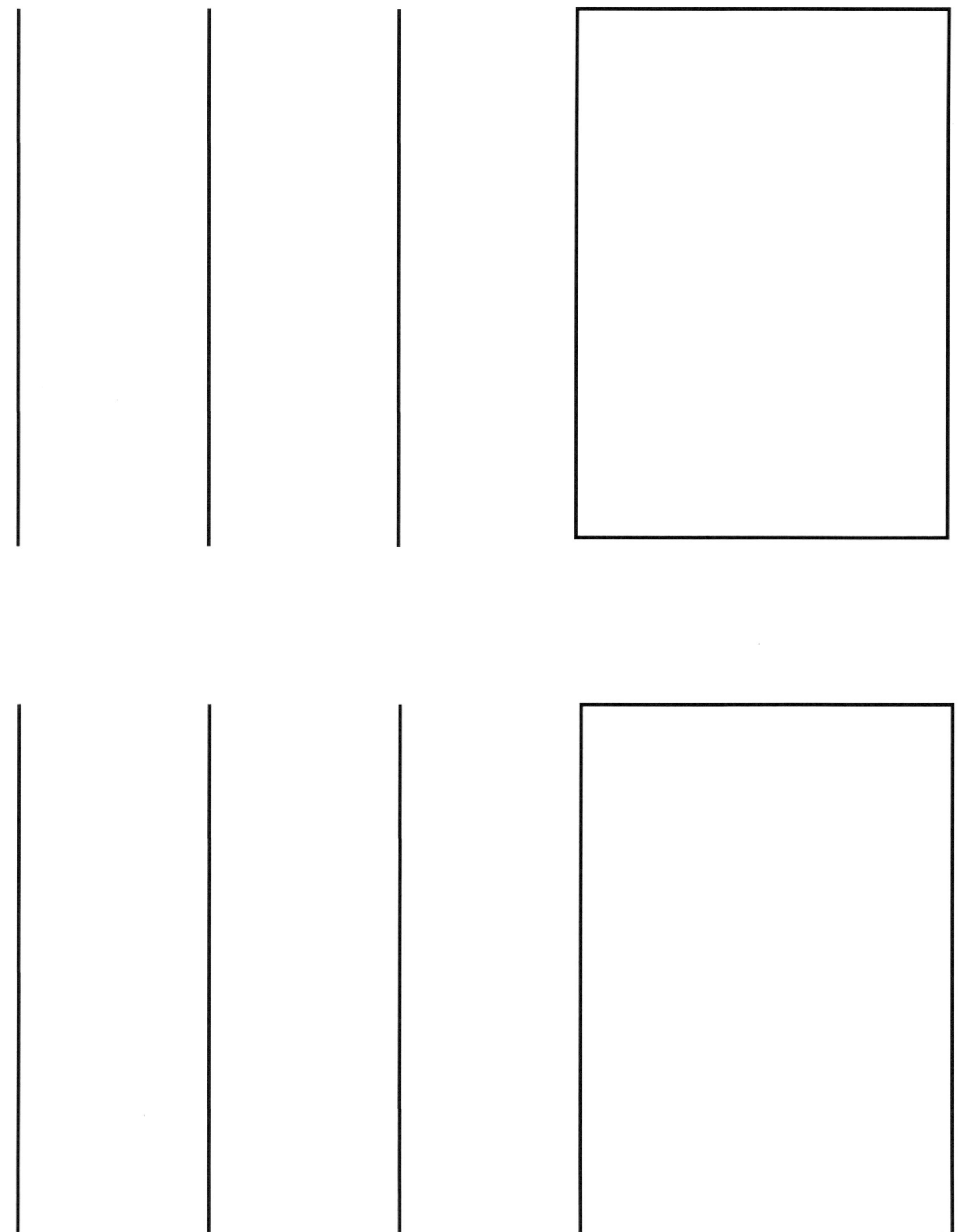

How To

Title
Instructions in Numbered Order
"You Will Need" List
Use First, Next/Then, & Last

Written By: _____

Date: _____

You Will Need:

• _____
• _____
• _____
• _____
• _____

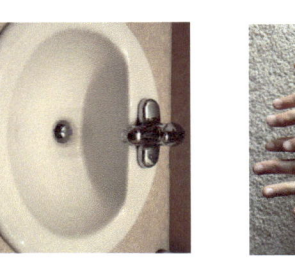

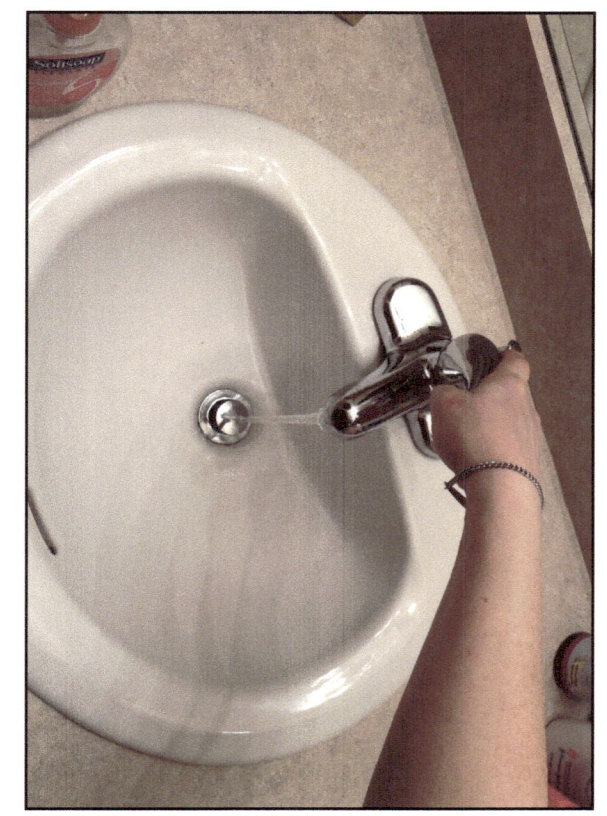

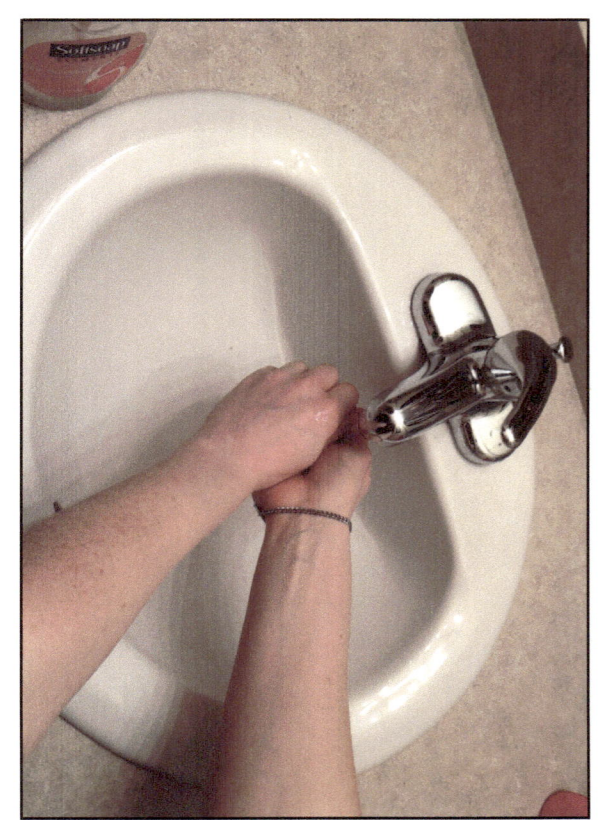

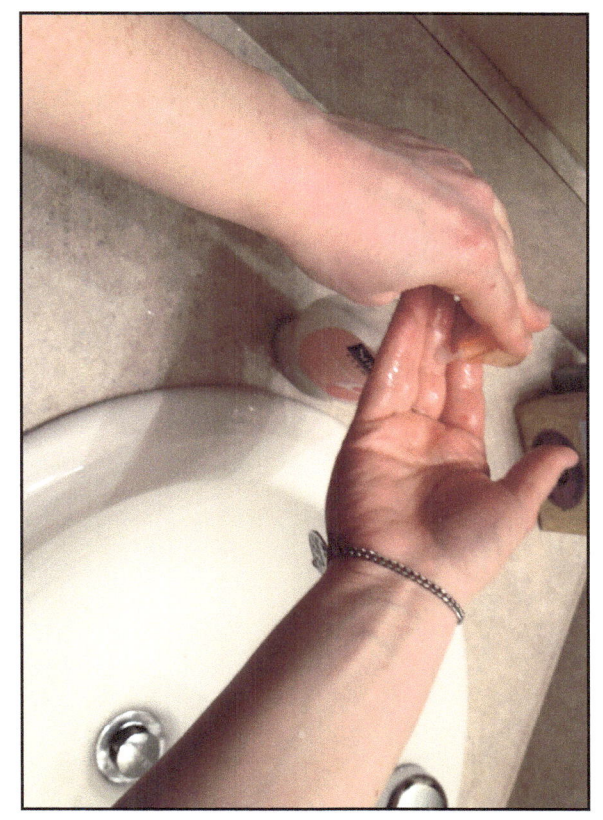

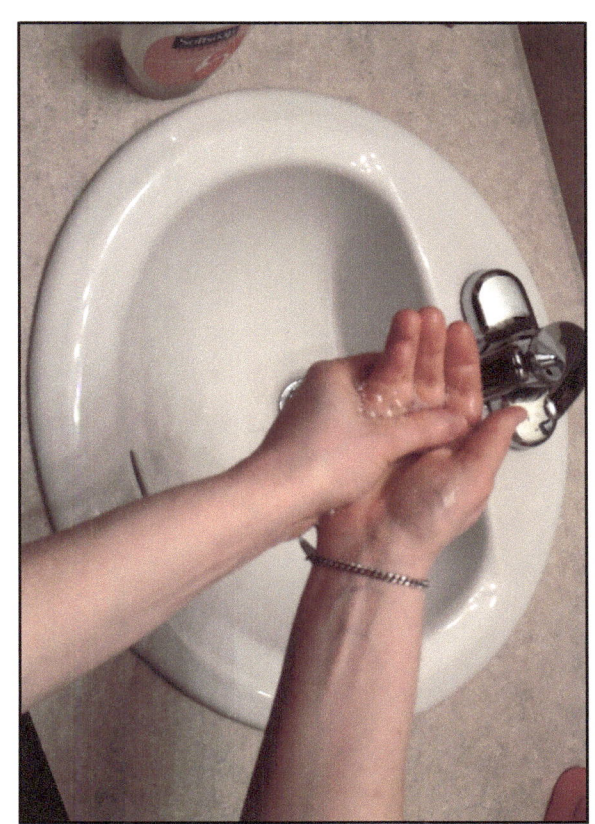

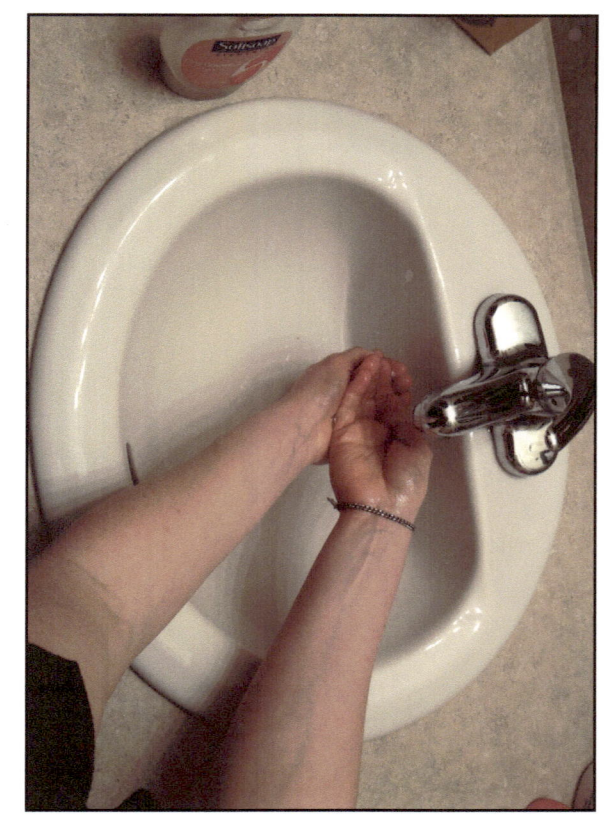

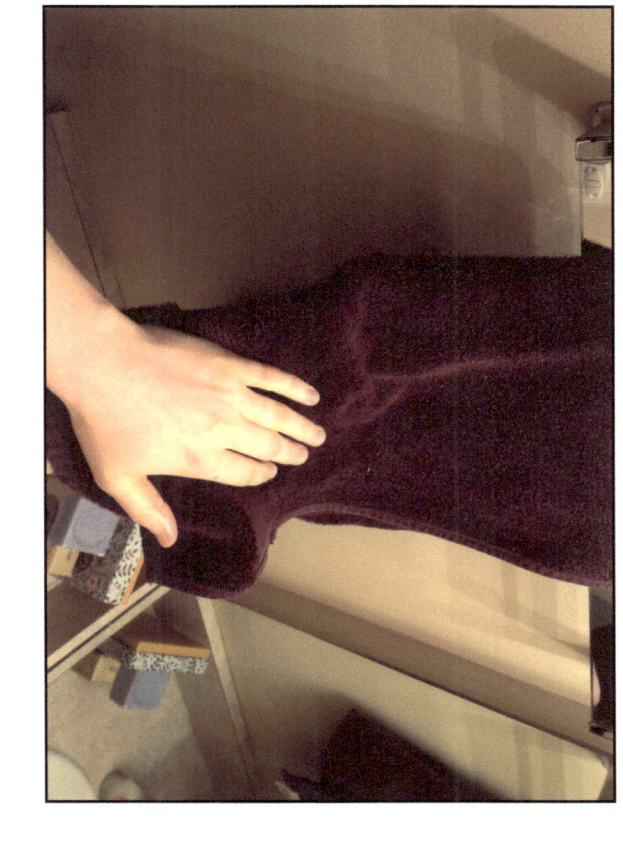

Author: _____ Peer Advisor: _____

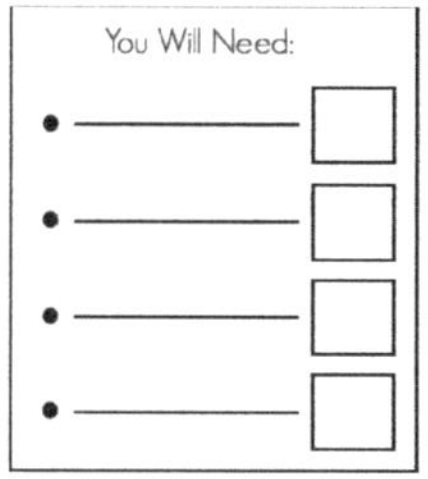

"You Will Need" List ☐

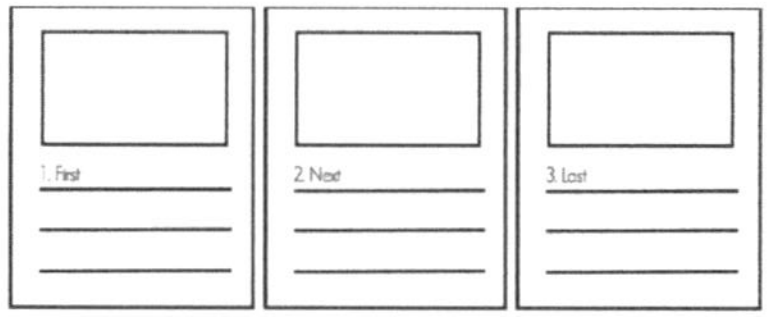

Title ☐

Instructions in Numbered ☐

Use First, Next/Then, & Last ☐

Author: _____ Peer Advisor: _____

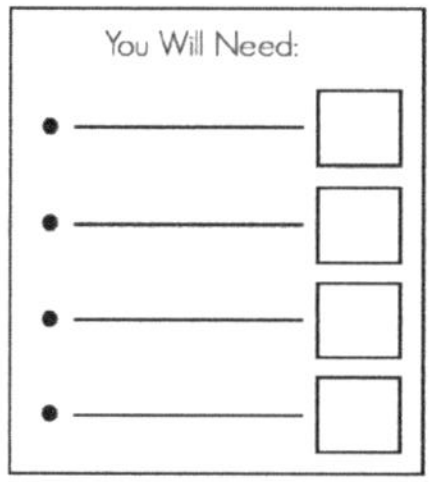

"You Will Need" List ☐

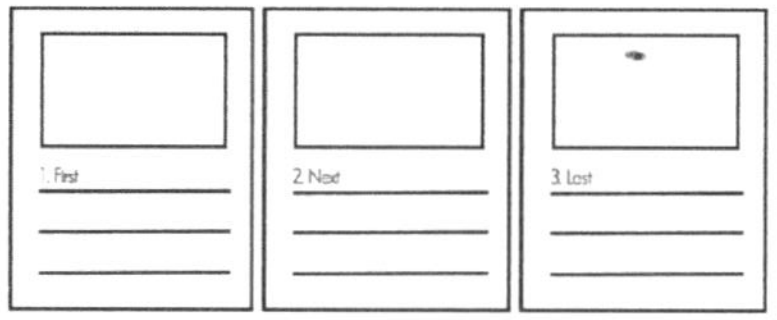

Title ☐

Instructions in Numbered ☐

Use First, Next/Then, & Last ☐

Title

You Will Need" List

Instructions in Numbered Order

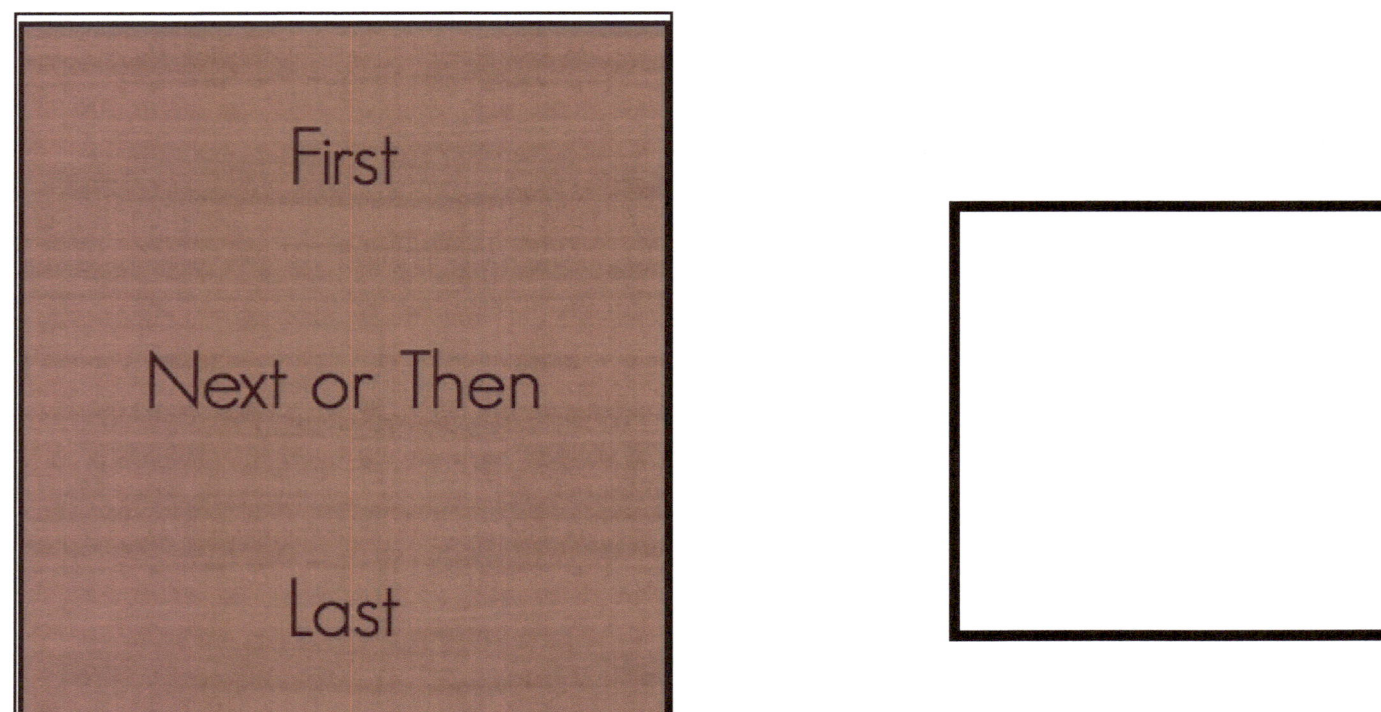

Use First, Next/Then, and Last

"HOW TO" MENTOR TEXTS

How To Make A Peanut Butter and Jelly Sandwich

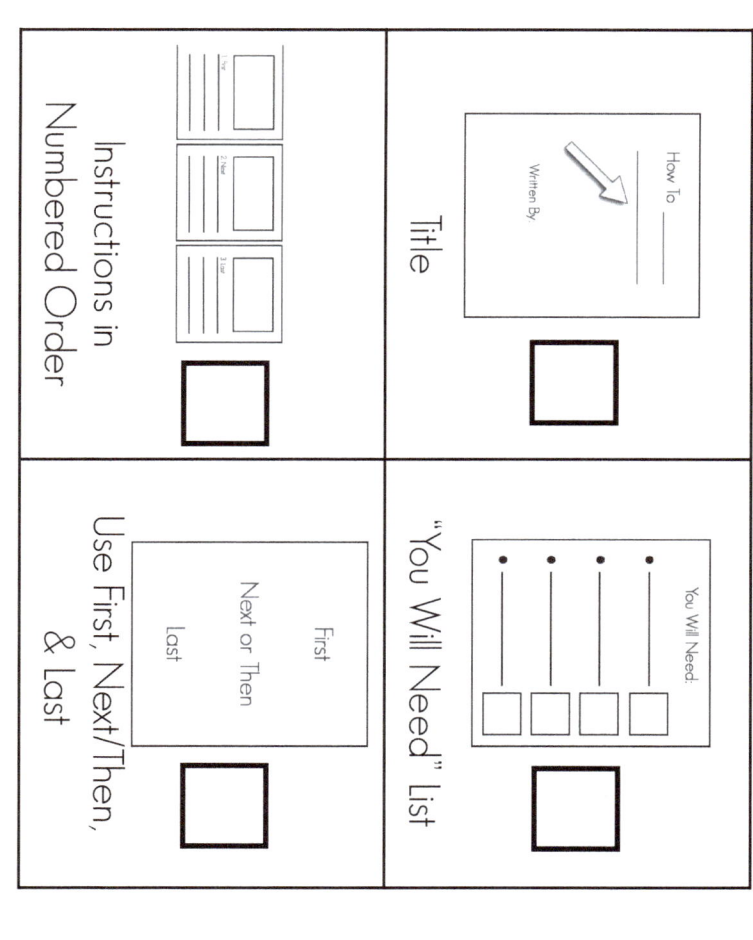

Written By: John Smith
Date: 5-10-15

You Will Need:

- a plate
- a knife
- peanut butter
- jelly
- two slices of bread

1. First, put the two slices of bread open faced on the plate.

2. Next, use the knife to spread peanut butter on both slices of bread.

3. Next, use the knife to spread jelly on both slices of bread, on top of the peanut butter.

4. Then, put both slices of bread together, gooey side in.

5. Last, eat the sandwich. Enjoy!

How To Play "Memory"

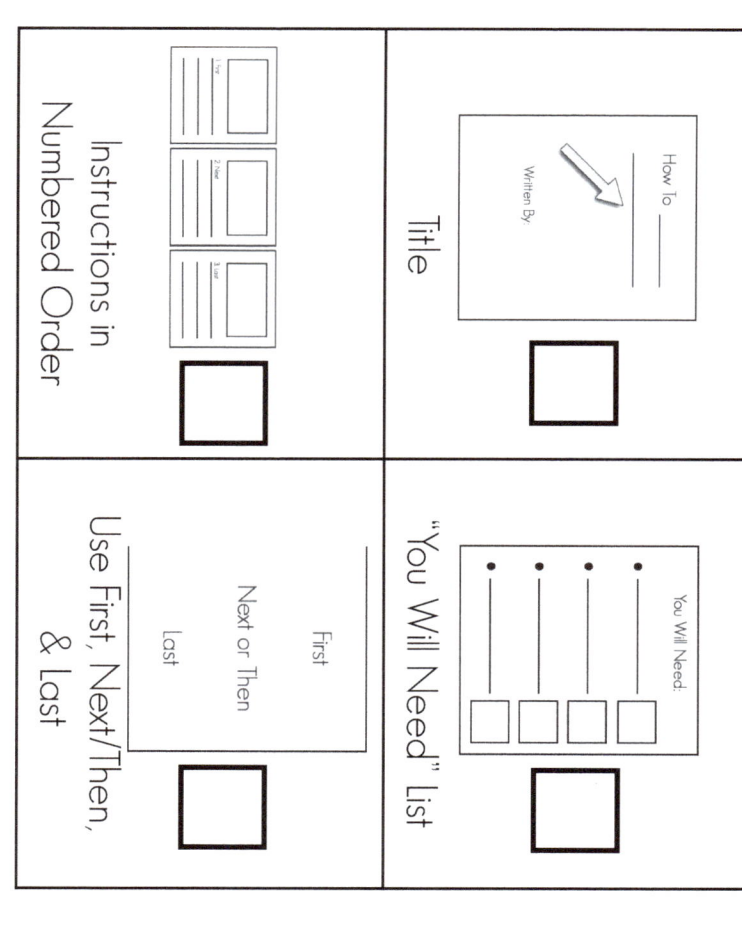

Written By: Jane Smith
Date: 5-10-15

You Will Need:

- a Memory game
- two players
- a clear place to play
-
-

1. First, mix up all the cards.

2. Next, line up the cards face down in neat rows.

3. Next, one player turns two cards over, leaving them in their places.

4. If they do not match, turn the cards back face down.

5. If you do find a match, pick up both cards and keep them. This player can go again.

6. Then repeat this process, taking turns, until all the pairs of cards have been picked up.

7. Last, both players count up all of their pairs. The player with the most pairs wins!

How To Do A Somersault

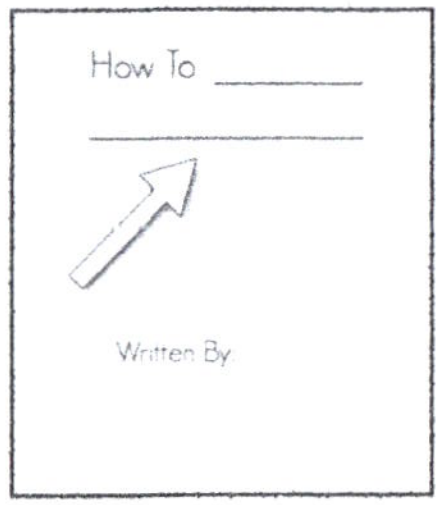 ☐ Title	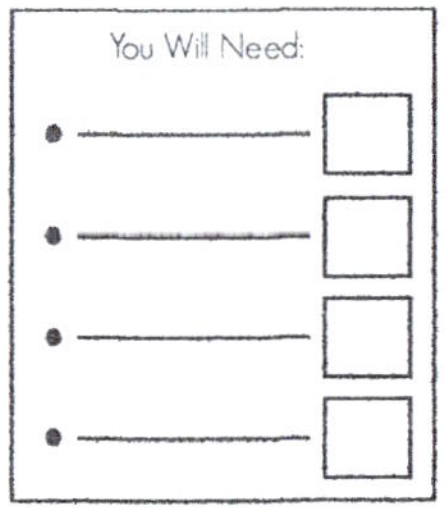 ☐ "You Will Need" List
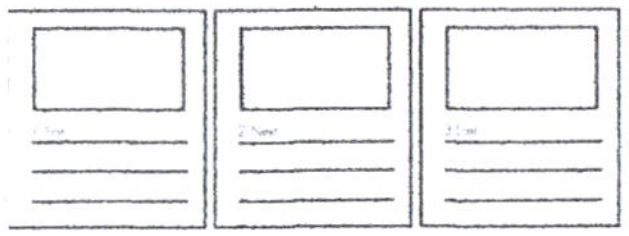 ☐ Instructions in Numbered Order	 ☐ Use First, Next/Then, & Last

Written By: Jane Smith

Date: 2-29-12

You Will Need:

- your body 
- clear floor space 
- ☐
- ☐
- ☐

1. First, stand with your legs slightly apart at one end of the floor space.

2. Next, put your hands on the floor and tuck your head between them.

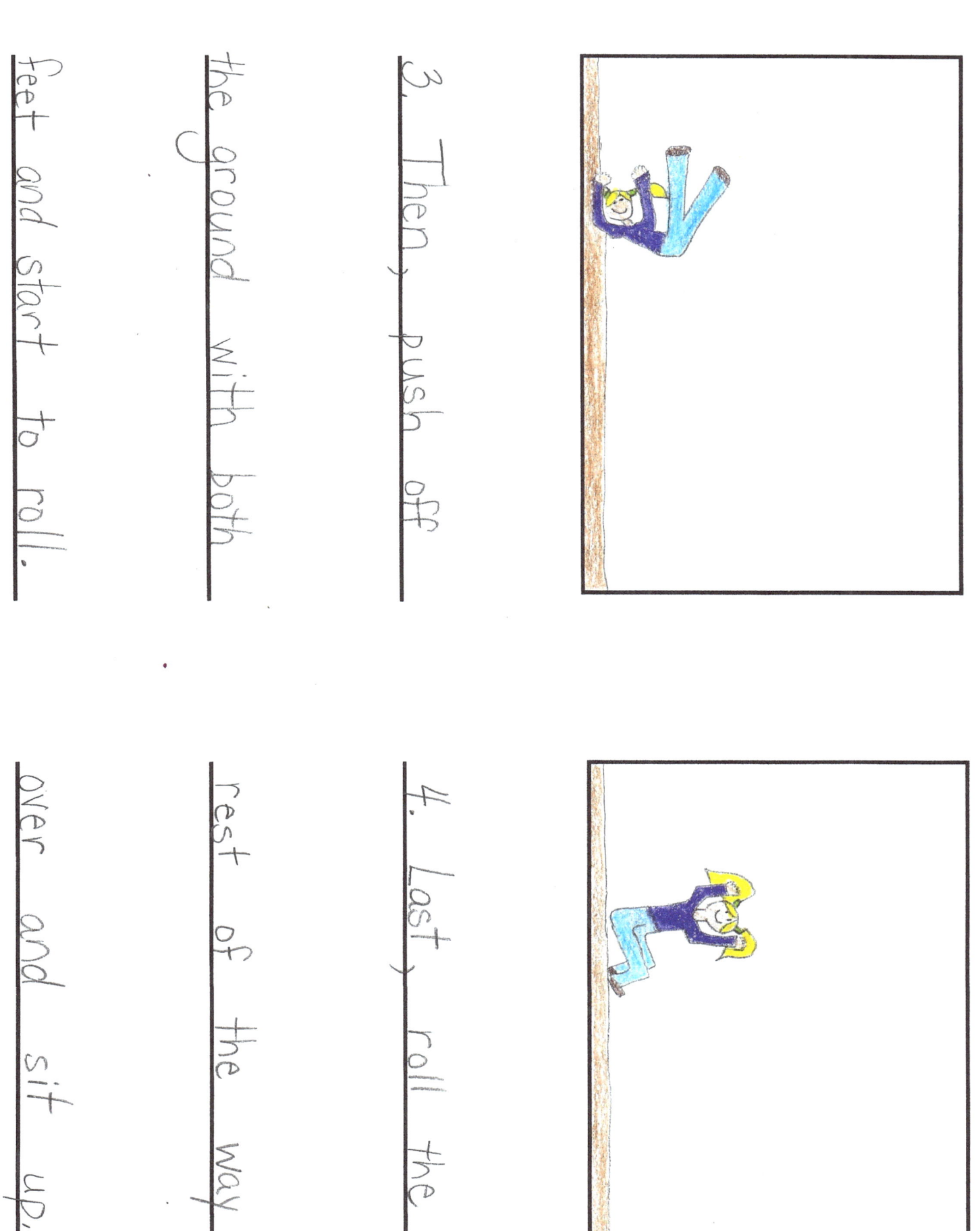

3. Then, push off the ground with both feet and start to roll.

4. Last, roll the rest of the way over and sit up.

How To Make A Delicious Smoothie

Title	Instructions in Numbered Order
"You Will Need" List	Use First, Next/Then, & Last

Written By: Jane Smith

Date: 2-2-12

You Will Need:

- a Blender
- Orange Juice
- Strawberries
- ice
- measuring cups

You Will Need:

-
-
-
- a glass
- a banana

1. First, pour one cup of orange juice in to the blender.

2. Next, pour one half cup of strawberries in to the blender.

3. Then, put one half of a banana in to the blender.

4. Next, put one and one half cups of ice cubes in to the blender.

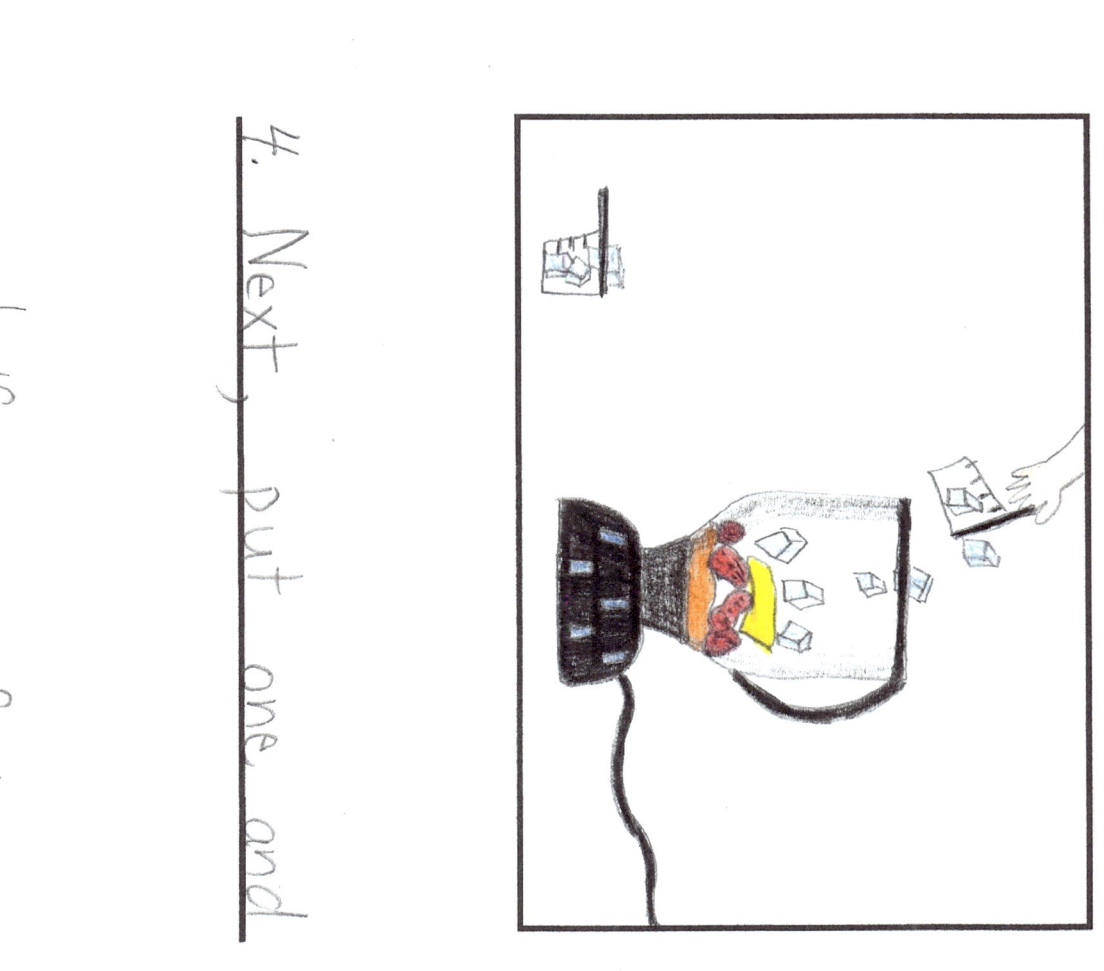

5. Next, turn the blender on and mix the contents of the blender.

6. Then, turn the blender off.

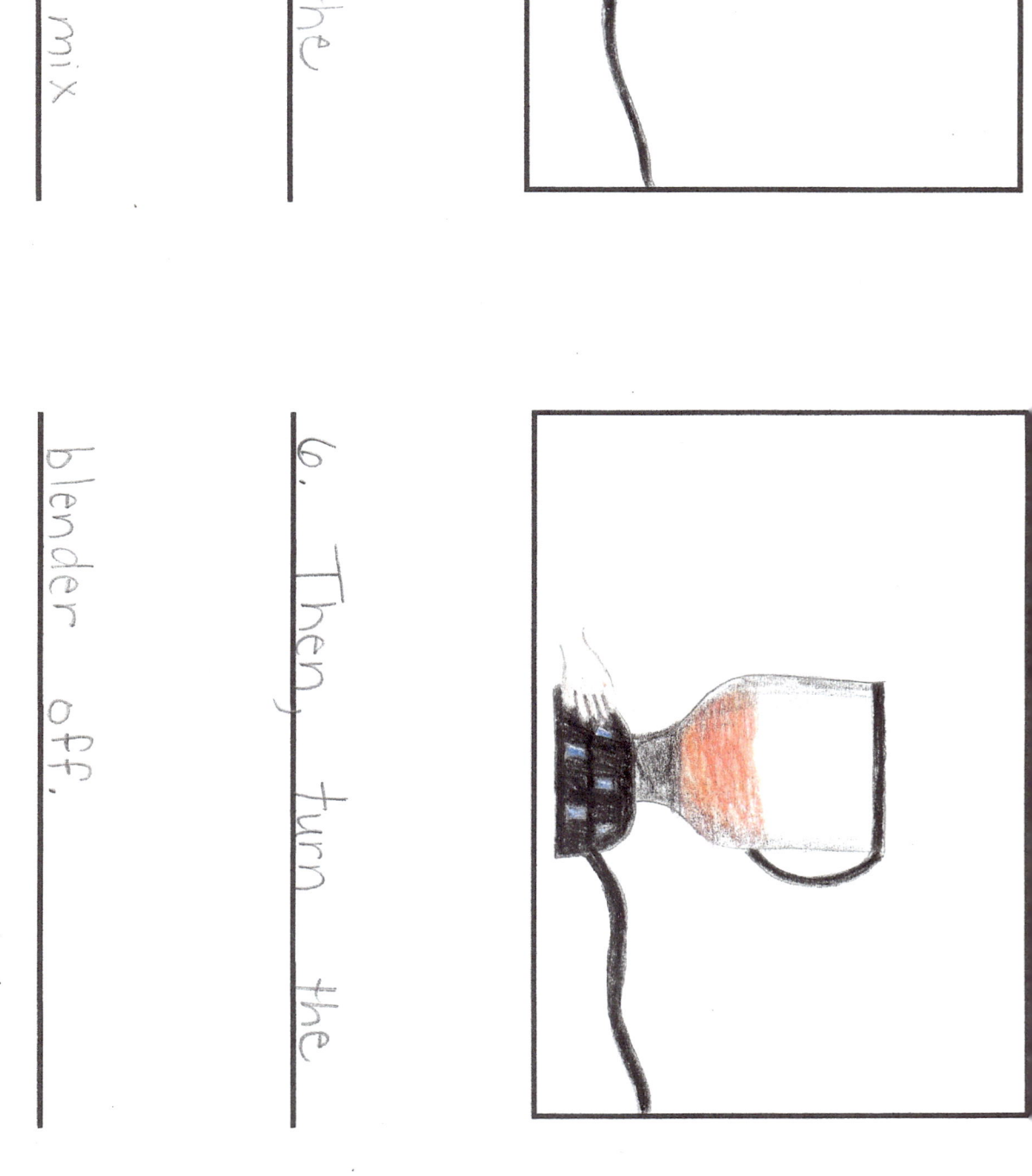

7. Next, pour the smoothie in to the glass.

8. Drink the smoothie and enjoy!

"If you get stuck on something and you don't know what to write about, you can think of what you're writing about. And think, if it's a true story, you can think of actually what happened and think of the pictures."

~ Lauren, age 7

"ALL ABOUT" BOOKS

BASIC CONCEPTS WITH MENTOR TEXT

Pacing Guide

Lesson/Activity Description	Time
Immersion: Read and expose students to many examples of "all about" books. While "how to" books are also great informational texts, be careful to immerse your students specifically in "all about" books for this unit. Model how readers do not always read informational texts from cover to cover. Rather, they use the table of contents to find what they are interested in, and bounce around throughout the book. Be sure to call your students' attention to nonfiction text features (table of contents, headings, diagrams, index, references). Use these terms regularly so that your students become very familiar with them. This should take place while you are wrapping up the previous unit (publishing, celebrating, etc.) It will happen during your read aloud portion of the day, not writing workshop.	One Week
Close Study: Choose your favorite "all about" book example from those that you worked with in the previous week - this book should be a good example of how you want the kids to write. Take a closer look again at the informational text features, noticing what good "all about" books have.	1 Day
Checklist Introduction: Show the children that you used the discussion you had as a class to develop a checklist for writers that are writing "all about" books. Explain that all "all about" books should have a title, true information about the topic, and a reference page.	1 Day
How to Write an All About Book: Explain to the kids that they will soon begin writing their own "all about" books. Show them the "How To Make An All About Book" poster (pages included in this packet) to explain the process.	$\frac{1}{2}$ Day

Pacing Guide

Lesson/Activity Description	Time
<u>Topic Lists Part 1</u>: Step 1 in writing an "all about" book is to make a list of possible topics you could write about. Demonstrate this as a large group. Compile a class list of topics that you could write about as a group. Science and social studies topics are great for this. Some ideas include: all about dogs, all about our school, all about airplanes, etc. This list should highlight topics that would ultimately make good "all about" books, which all the kids can relate to. This is a good time to discourage ideas that are "how to" books (how to tie your shoes, how to take care of a hamster). "How To" writing is a separate unit.	1 Day
<u>Group Written All About Book</u>: I recommend writing the first "all about" book together as a class. Take your students through the 8 step process, using one of the ideas you came up with on your topics list. I do this as my writing time each day for a few days. Sometimes the kids share the pen, and sometimes I write, but they are involved in researching and developing ideas. I use a large, laminated book for this, which I can then reuse. I included photos in this packet. You could also use a paper book, or overhead slides.	2-3 Days
<u>Topics Lists Part 2</u>: Now it is finally time to let the kids start the writing process on their own! Spend one day entirely devoted to developing topic ideas lists. Before sending them off, I like to feed their ideas a little, to let them know that a wide variety of ideas are acceptable. I might say, "I know _____ knows all about tractors, _____ knows all about Batman's special tools, and _____ is interested in horses." This tends to fuel the motivation some more! Have the kids write their own topic ideas list, which will remain in their folder for the whole unit.	1 Day

Pacing Guide

Lesson/Activity Description	Time
<u>Minilessons:</u> The next portion of the unit will involve student work and minilessons as needed. I start every day with a quick review of the "How To Make An All About Book" poster, as students will be moving through the steps at their own pace. One student might be revising their second book while another student is doing the references page of their first. As long as they know the steps, this is fine! This is a time when you could use the blank page mentor text (included in this unit) to have the kids help you write, or you could use this text for a small group of kids who need extra support. For young writers I recommend having booklets pre-made. The booklet paper in this pack can be printed back to back to save paper. ** The booklet paper pages are intentionally not perfectly centered on the page. This is to allow for a slight margin where the book is stapled. **	2 Weeks
<u>Peer Revision:</u> Have students select a piece that they would like to publish. Then have them work with a partner, using the peer checklist, to revise and edit their work.	1 Day
<u>Publishing:</u> Have students revise and edit their chosen piece, using the feedback from their writing partners. They can then come to you for feedback. (Begin immersion in next unit).	1-3 Days
<u>Celebration:</u> Share the published pieces with an audience and celebrate!	1 Day

A Note About Mentor Texts: In this unit, having a large selection of mentor texts is critical. If you head to the nonfiction section of the library, you will have more than enough texts to choose from. Just be careful not to get "how to" books at this stage. "How to" books are structured differently, and the features should not be confused with those found in "all about" books.

Anchor Tools

How To Write An "All About" Book Poster Example
(use pages 8-21 to build your own)

Large Group Wipe Off All About Book
(for group written all about book)

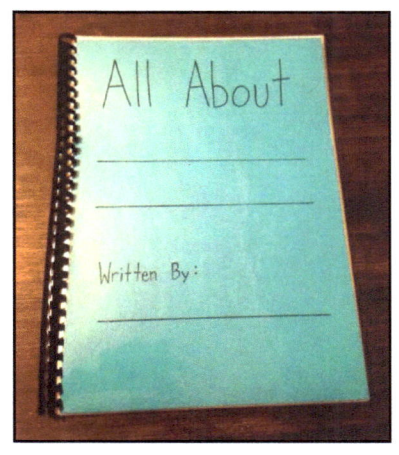

Sample of Booklet Paper Possibilities
(copy, cut and staple, or have your students collate and staple their own booklets)

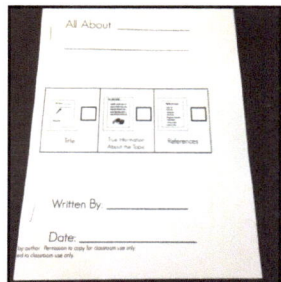
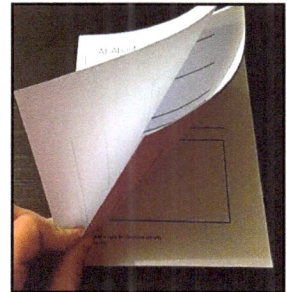

1. Brainstorm a list of possible topics.

2. Choose one topic.

3. Research your topic.

4. Write the title.

5. Write the words and draw or glue the pictures for each page of the book. Include true information and helpful pictures or diagrams.

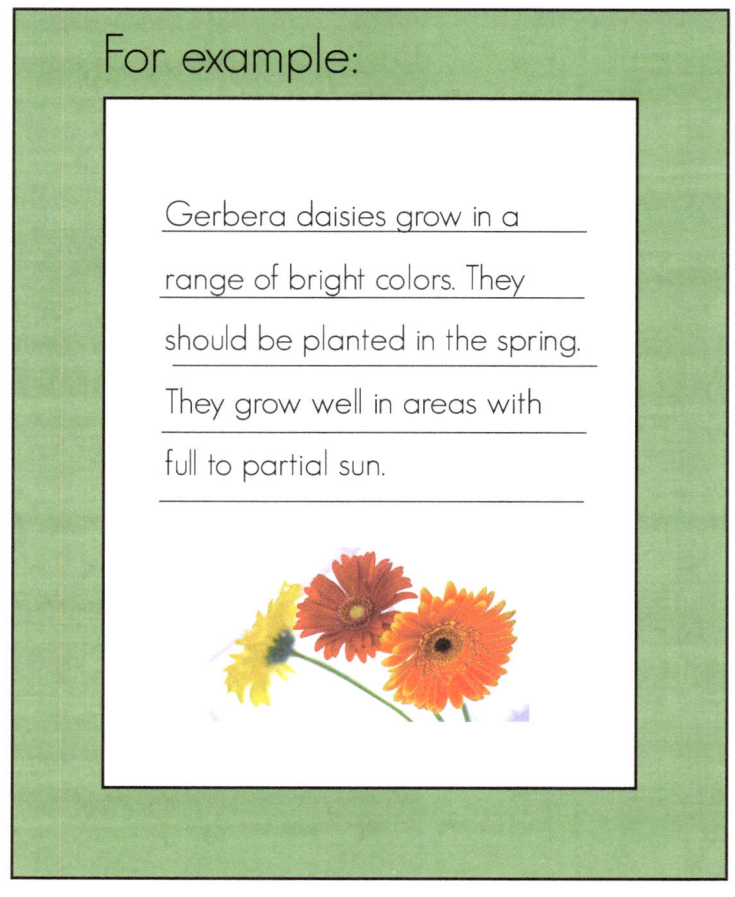

6. Write the names and information about your sources on the references page.

References:

- Book Title
- Book Title
- Internet Site
- Internet Site
- Magazine article title
- Documentary
- Interview Notes
- Journal Article

7. Revise using the checklist.

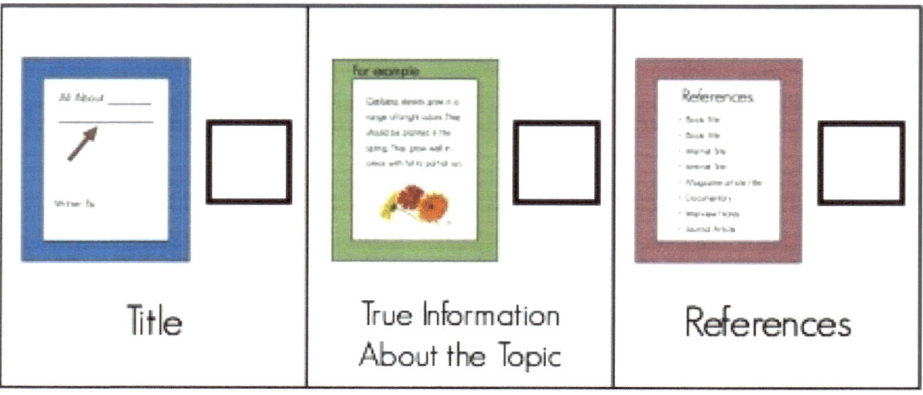

8. Start over at step 2.

Name _____

Topic Ideas:

- _____

- _____

- _____

- _____

- _____

All About _____

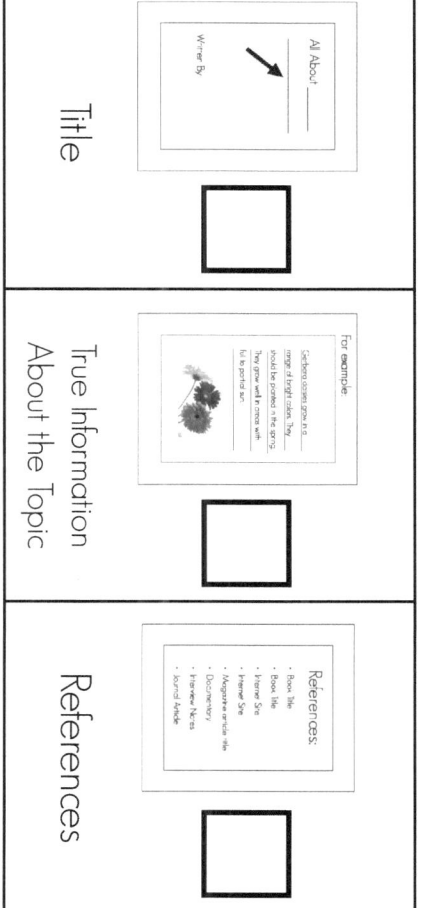

Written By: _____

Date: _____

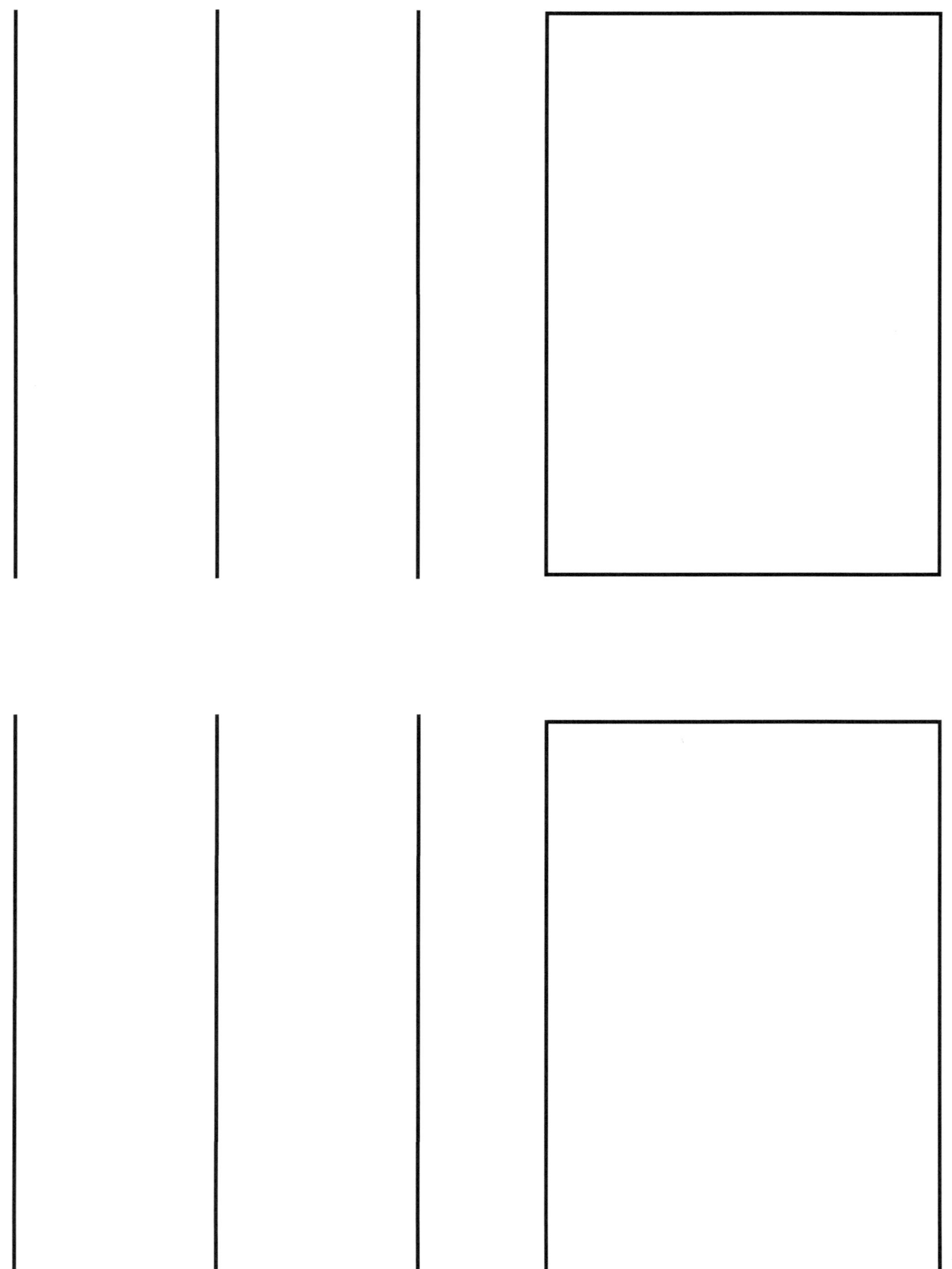

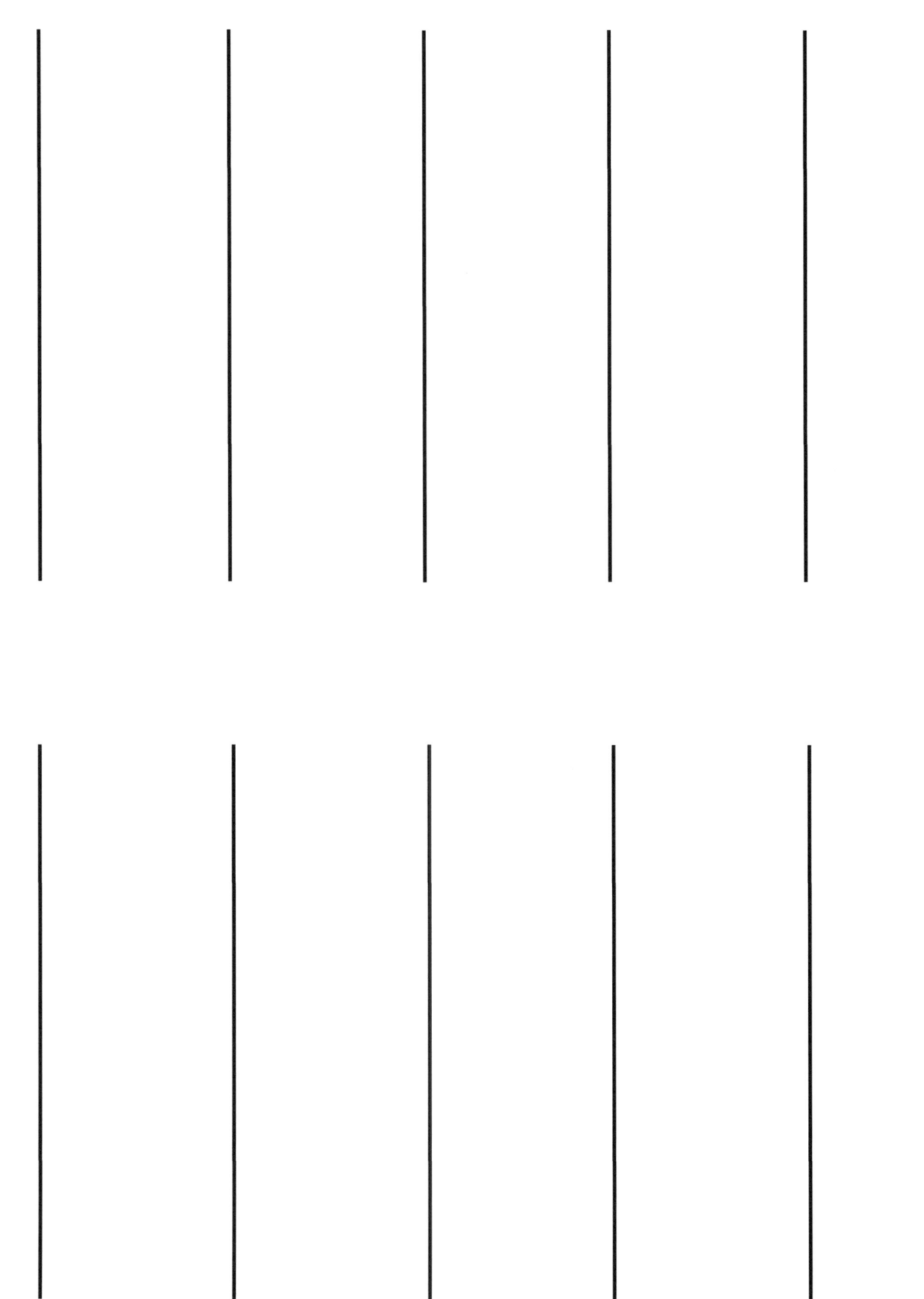

References

References

All About _____
Beagles

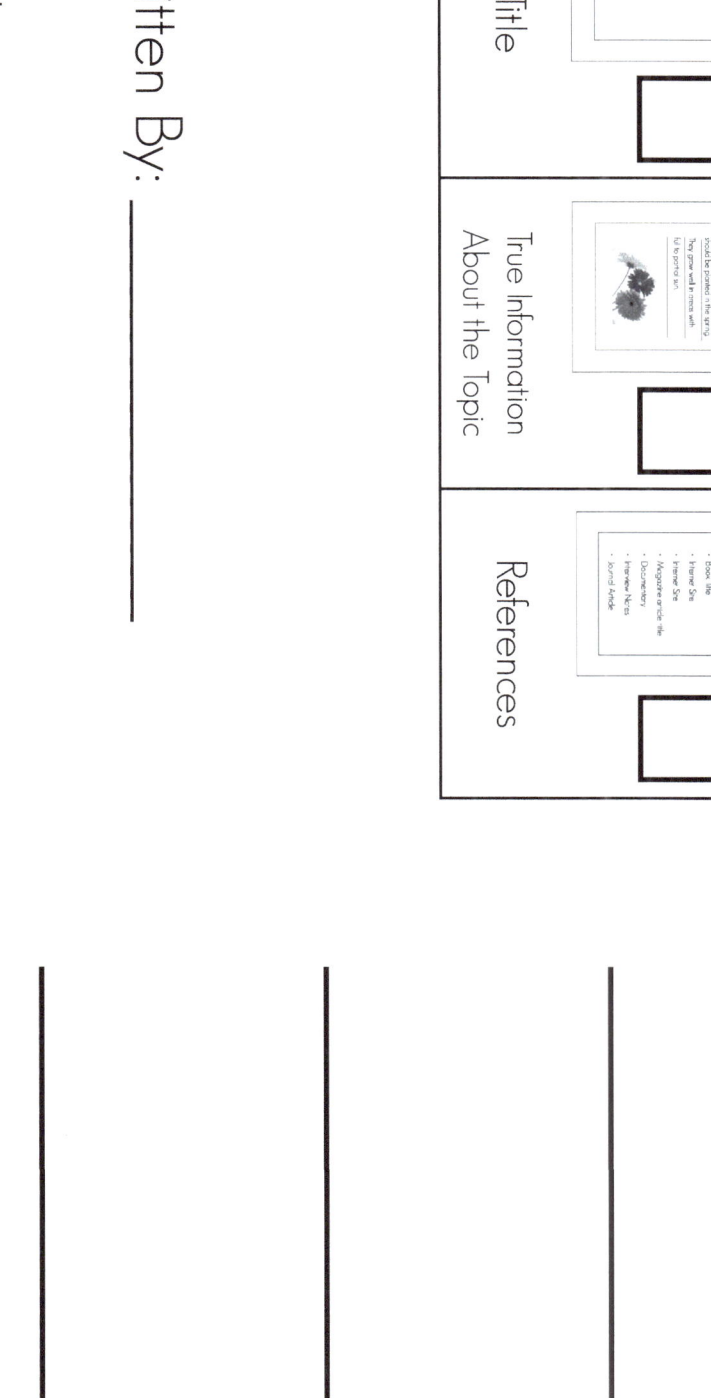

Written By: _____

Date: _____

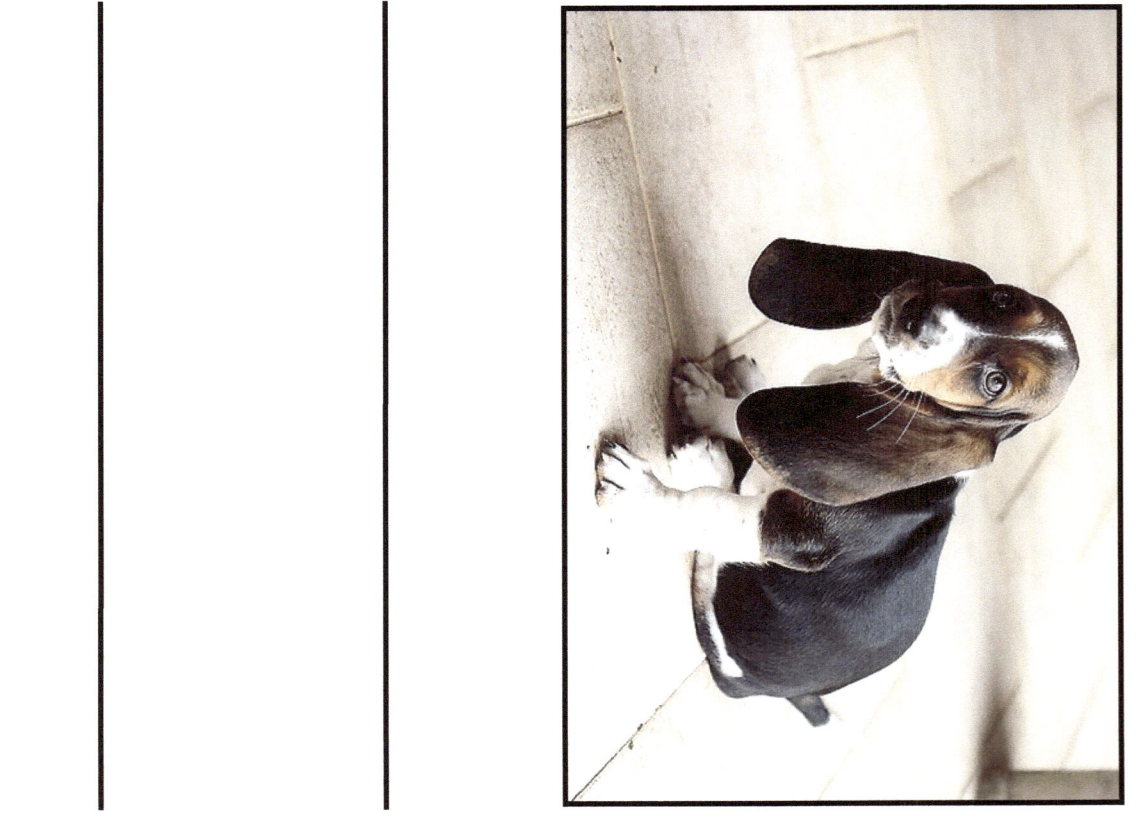

References

All About Beagles

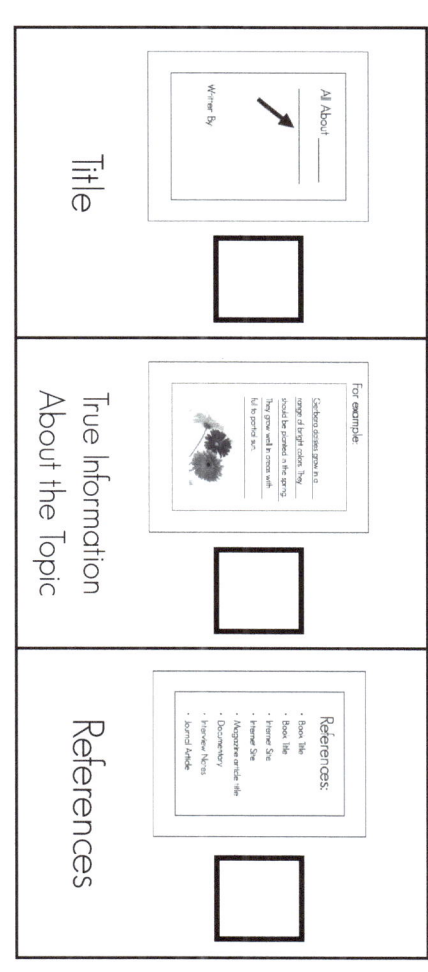

| Title | True Information About the Topic | References |

Beagle puppies require patient, firm training. They also need to have regular exercise to help them remain calm.

Written By: Karen Langdon

Date: 8/12/16

Playing tracking games and purchasing animal scents will help satisfy the beagle puppy's hunting instinct.

The average size of a litter of beagle puppies is seven, with a range of two to fourteen. They come in many colors, including tricolor, red and white, and lemon.

Once a beagle is full grown, a male will weigh between 22 and 25 pounds, and a female will weigh between 20 and 23 pounds.

Beagle puppies require their mother's milk until they are eight weeks old. Solid food can be introduced at four weeks

of age. Beagles need a diet of 35-40% meat, 25-35% vegetables, and some starch. Pasta is a healthy option for a beagle.

Beagles are popular hunting dogs. They have a cheerful personality as well. They are social dogs that like to be

around people and other dogs. Beagles are easygoing and playful dogs. They are curious and fun loving!

If you want a purebred beagle, you might need to purchase your dog through a breeder. There are many

dogs available in animal shelters as well.

You might just find a beagle!

References

- http://www.beaglepro.com/Feeding.html
- http://www.dogbreedinfo.com/beagle.htm
- http://wwwwoofipedia.com/discover/breeds/beagle
- https://www.akc.org/breeds/beagle/index.cfm

Author: _____ Peer Advisor: _____

Title

☐

True Information About the Topic

☐

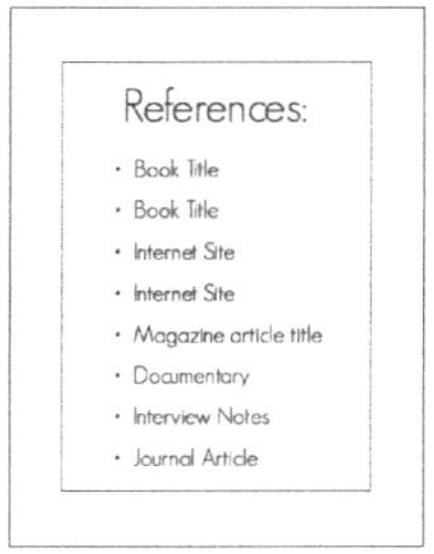

References

☐

Author: _____ Peer Advisor: _____

Title

☐

True Information About the Topic

☐

References

☐

Title

References

True Information About the Topic

1. Brainstorm a list of possible topics.

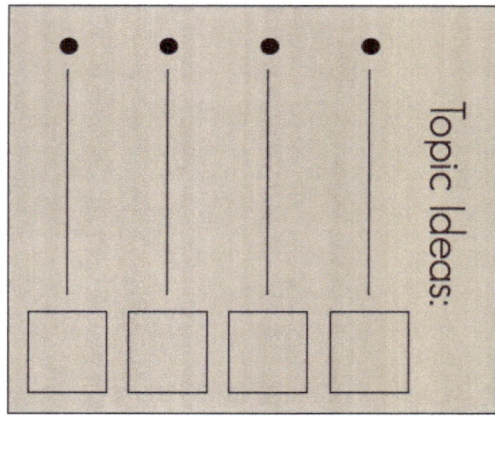

Topic Ideas:

2. Choose one topic.

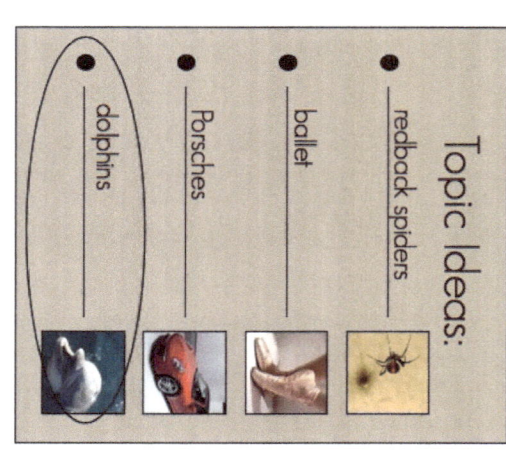

Topic Ideas:
- redback spiders
- ballet
- Porsches
- dolphins

3. Research your topic.

4. Write the title.

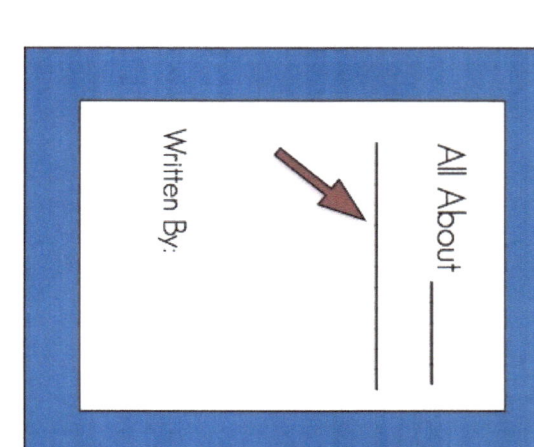

All About ____
Written By:

5. Write the words and draw or glue the pictures for each page of the book. Include true information and helpful pictures or diagrams.

For example:

Gerbera daisies grow in a range of bright colors. They should be planted in the spring. They grow well in areas with full to partial sun.

6. Write the names and information about your sources on the references page.

References:
- Book Title
- Book Title
- Internet Site
- Internet Site
- Magazine article title
- Documentary
- Interview Notes
- Journal Article

7. Revise using the checklist.

title
True Information About the Topic
References

8. Start over at step 2.

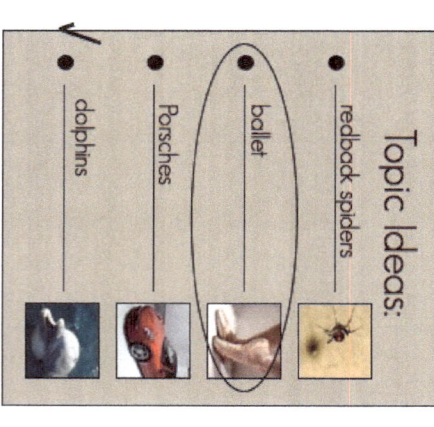

Topic Ideas:
- redback spiders
- ballet
- Porsches
- dolphins

"ALL ABOUT" BOOKS
ADVANCED CONCEPTS

Pacing Guide

Lesson/Activity Description	Time
Immersion: Read and expose students to many examples of "all about" books. While "how to" books are also great informational texts, be careful to immerse your students specifically in "all about" books for this unit. Model how readers do not always read informational texts from cover to cover. Rather, they use the table of contents to find what they are interested in, and bounce around throughout the book. Be sure to call your students' attention to nonfiction text features (table of contents, headings, diagrams, index, references). Use these terms regularly so that your students become very familiar with them. This should take place while you are wrapping up the previous unit (publishing, celebrating, etc.) It will happen during your read aloud portion of the day, not writing workshop.	One Week
Close Study: Choose your favorite "all about" book example from those that you worked with in the previous week - this book should be a good example of how you want the kids to write. Take a closer look again at the informational text features, noticing what good "all about" books have.	1 Day
Checklist Introduction: Show the children that you used the discussion you had as a class to develop a checklist for writers that are writing "all about" books. Explain that all "all about" books should have a title, a table of contents, headings, true information about the topic, and a reference page.	1 Day
How to Write an All About Book: Explain to the kids that they will soon begin writing their own "all about" books. Show them the "How To Make An All About Book" poster (pages included in this packet) to explain the process.	½ Day

Pacing Guide

Lesson/Activity Description	Time
Topic Lists Part 1: Step 1 in writing an "all about" book is to make a list of possible topics you could write about. Demonstrate this as a large group. Compile a class list of topics that you could write about as a group. Science and social studies topics are great for this. Some ideas include: all about dogs, all about our school, all about airplanes, etc. This list should highlight topics that would ultimately make good "all about" books, which all the kids can relate to. This is a good time to discourage ideas that are "how to" books (how to tie your shoes, how to take care of a hamster). "How To" writing is a separate unit.	1 Day
Group Written All About Book: I recommend writing the first "all about" book together as a class. Take your students through the 14 step process, using one of the ideas you came up with on your topics list. I do this as my writing time each day for a few days. Sometimes the kids share the pen, and sometimes I write, but they are involved in researching and developing ideas. I use a large, laminated book for this, which I can then reuse. I included photos in this packet. You could also use a paper book, or overhead slides.	2-3 Days
Topics Lists Part 2: Now it is finally time to let the kids start the writing process on their own! Spend one day entirely devoted to developing topic ideas lists. Before sending them off, I like to feed their ideas a little, to let them know that a wide variety of ideas are acceptable. might say, "I know _____ knows all about tractors, _____ knows all about Batman's special tools, and _____ is interested in horses." This tends to fuel the motivation some more! Have the kids write their own topic ideas list, which will remain in their folder for the whole unit.	1 Day

Pacing Guide

Lesson/Activity Description	Time
Minilessons: The next portion of the unit will involve student work and minilessons as needed. I often find the need to reteach the page numbering process, as the students are not used to leaving a page unfinished and going back to it later. I start every day with a quick review of the "How To Make An All About Book" poster, as students will be moving through the steps at their own pace. One student might be revising their second book while another student is doing the table of contents of their first. As long as they know the steps, this is fine! This is a time when you could use the blank page mentor text (included in this unit) to have the kids help you write, or you could use this text for a small group of kids who need extra support. You will need to spend some time with your students exploring the paper options. Because informational texts have headings and images, I have supplied a variety of choices. You could select one that you prefer and have pre-made booklets, or you could have piles of paper choices available for students to select and staple together. You will need to discuss why they might choose a certain page (ex: large image page versus one with a smaller image and some text), and you will need to plan some minilessons to teach them how to keep their pages organized as they work. ** The booklet paper pages are intentionally not perfectly centered on the page. This is to allow for a slight margin where the book is stapled. **	2 Weeks
Peer Revision: Have students select a piece that they would like to publish. Then have them work with a partner, using the peer checklist, to revise and edit their work.	1 Day
Publishing: Have students revise and edit their chosen piece, using the feedback from their writing partners. They can then come to you for feedback. (Begin immersion in next unit).	1-3 Days
Celebration: Share the published pieces with an audience and celebrate!	1 Day

A Note About Mentor Texts: In this unit, having a large selection of mentor texts is critical. If you head to the nonfiction section of the library, you will have more than enough texts to choose from. Just be careful not to get "how to" books at this stage. "How to" books are structured differently, and the features should not be confused with those found in "all about" books.

Anchor Tools

How To Write An "All About" Book Poster Example
(use pages 8-21 to build your own)

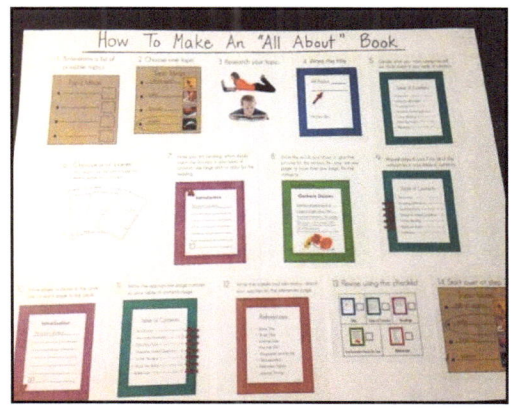

Large Group Wipe Off All About Book
(for group written all about book)

Sample of Booklet Paper Possibilities
(copy, cut and staple, or have your students collate and staple their own booklets)

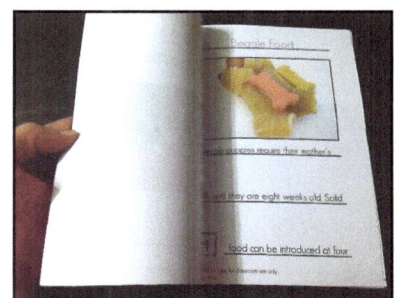

1. Brainstorm a list of possible topics.

2. Choose one topic.

3. Research your topic.

4. Write the title.

5. Decide what your main categories will be. Write these in your table of contents.

Table of Contents:

- Introduction ------------------------
- Interesting Information -------------
- Surprising Facts --------------------
- Frequently Asked Questions ---
- Further Reading --------------------
- About the Author ------------------
- References -----------------------------

6. Choose your paper.
You might use the same type for every page, or a variety.

7. Write your first heading, which should match the first item in your table of contents. Use large print or color for the heading.

8. Write the words and draw or glue the pictures for this section. You may use one page, or more than one page, for the category.

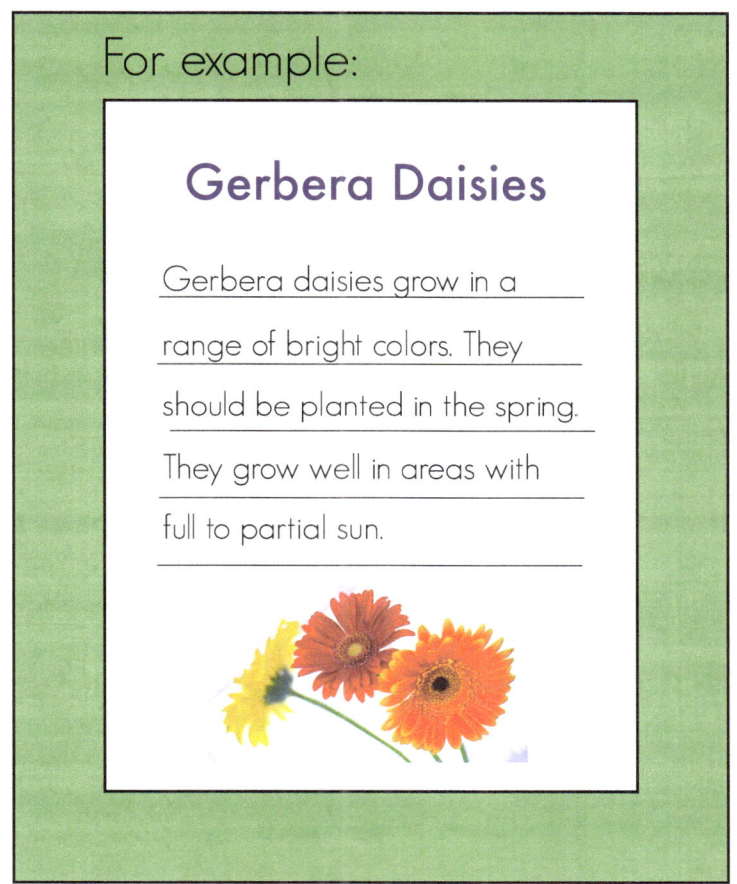

9. Repeat steps 7 and 8 for all of the categories in your table of contents.

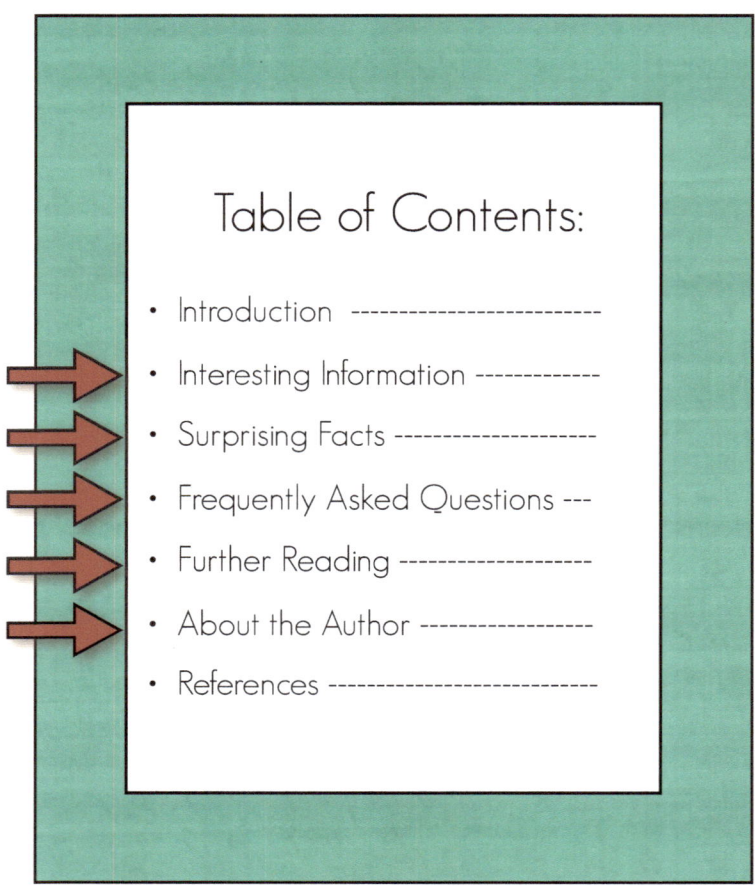

10. Write page numbers in the small box on each page in the book.

11. Write the appropriate page numbers on your table of contents page.

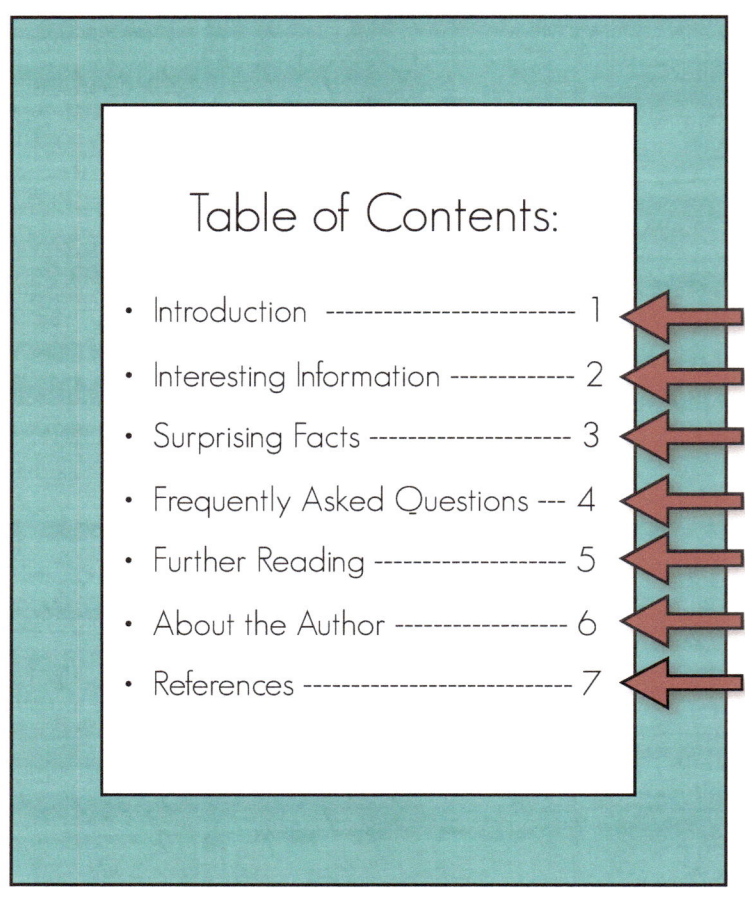

12. Write the names and information about your sources on the references page.

References:

- Book Title
- Book Title
- Internet Site
- Internet Site
- Magazine article title
- Documentary
- Interview Notes
- Journal Article

13. Revise using the checklist.

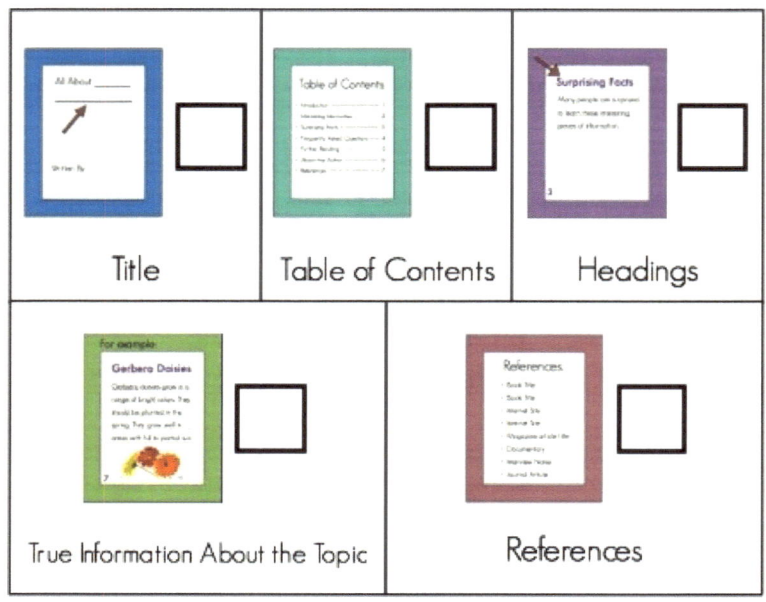

14. Start over at step 2.

Name _____

Topic Ideas:

- _____

- _____

- _____

- _____

- _____

All About _____

Title	Table of Contents	Headings

True Information About the Topic	References

Written By: _____

Date: _____

All About _____

Title	Table of Contents	Headings

True Information About the Topic	References

Written By: _____

Date: _____

Table of Contents:

- _____ Page ____
- _____ Page ____
- _____ Page ____
- _____ Page ____
- _____ Page ____
- _____ Page ____
- _____ Page ____
- _____ Page ____
- _____ Page ____

Table of Contents:

- _____ Page ____
- _____ Page ____
- _____ Page ____
- _____ Page ____
- _____ Page ____
- _____ Page ____
- _____ Page ____
- _____ Page ____
- _____ Page ____
- _____ Page ____

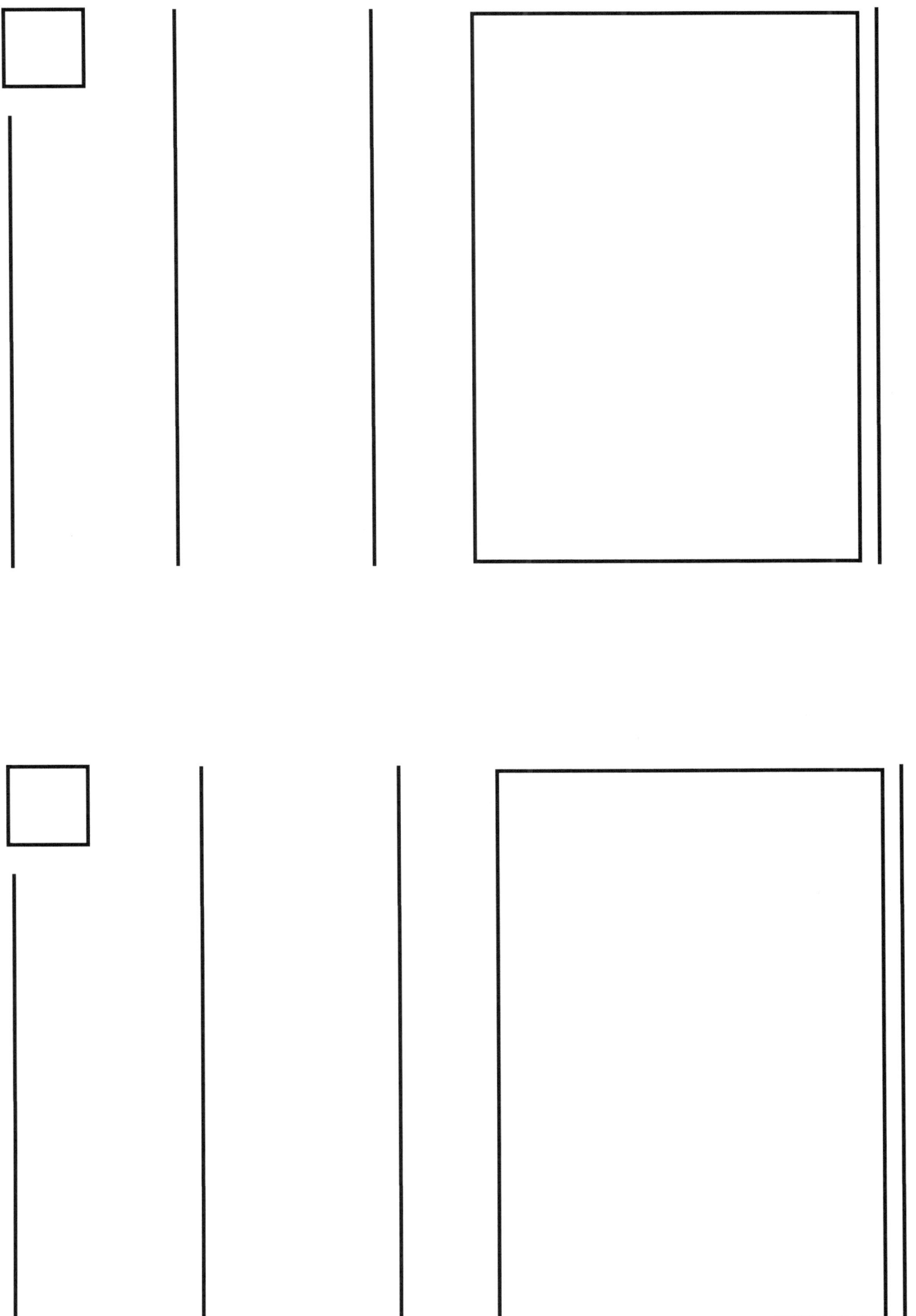

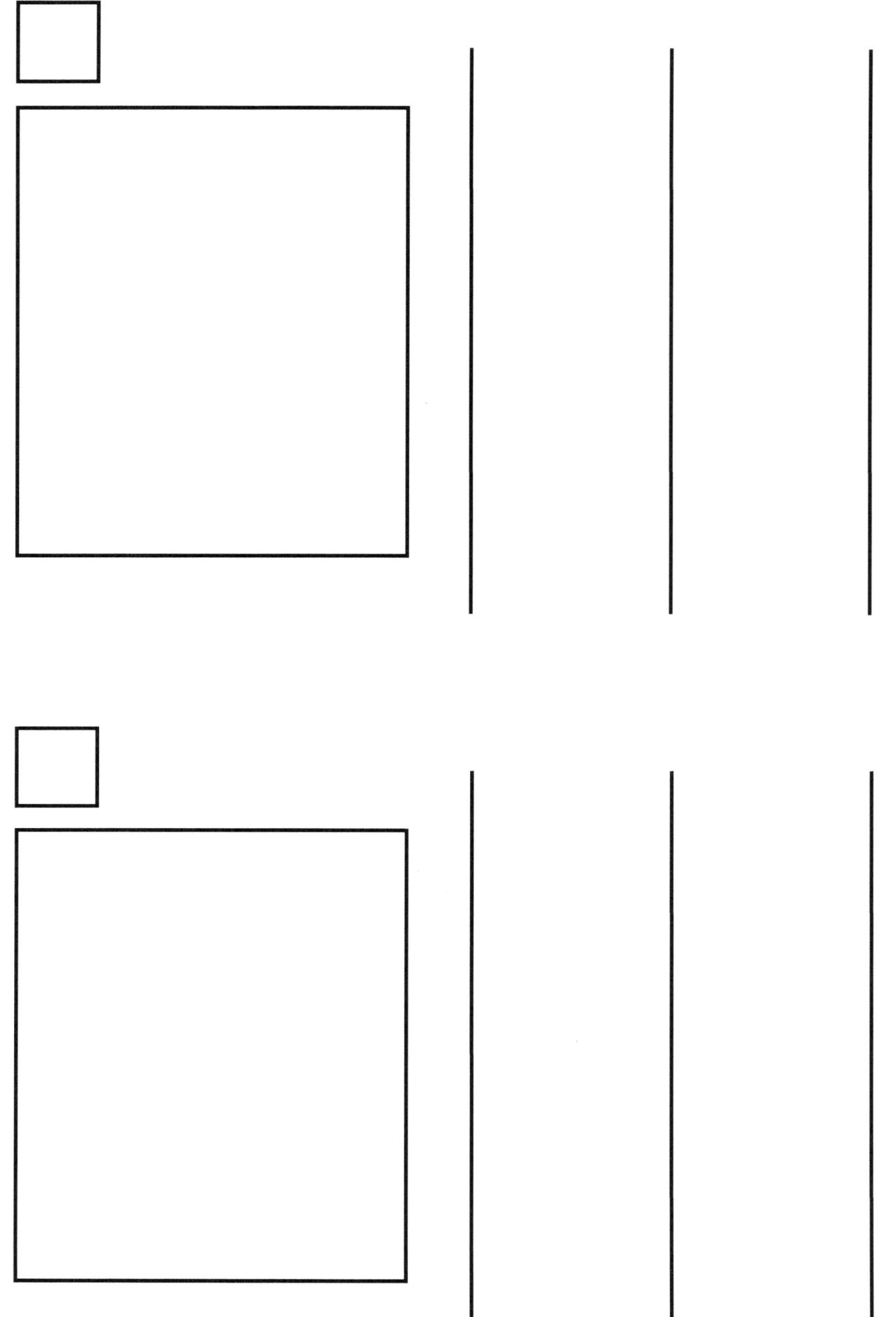

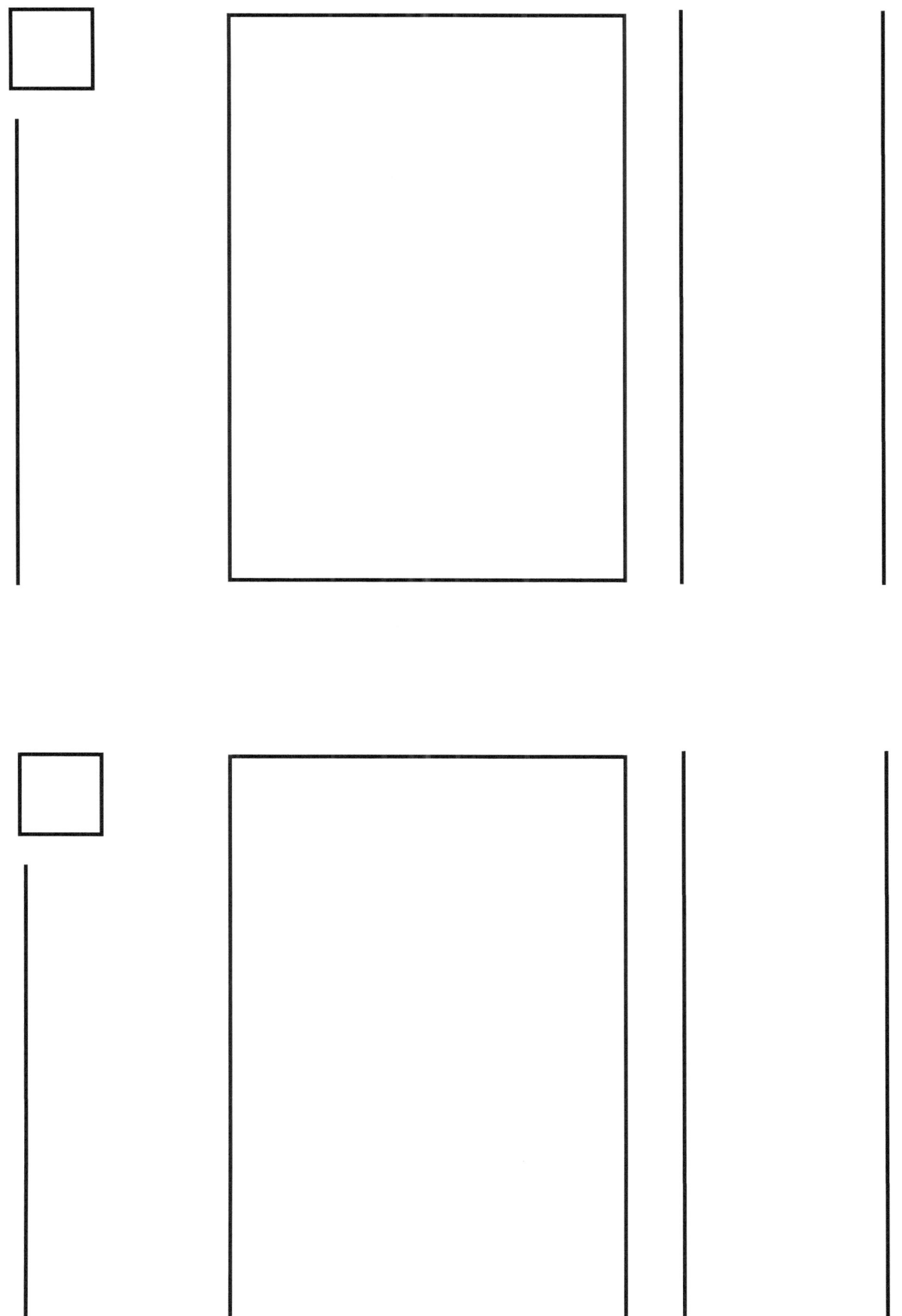

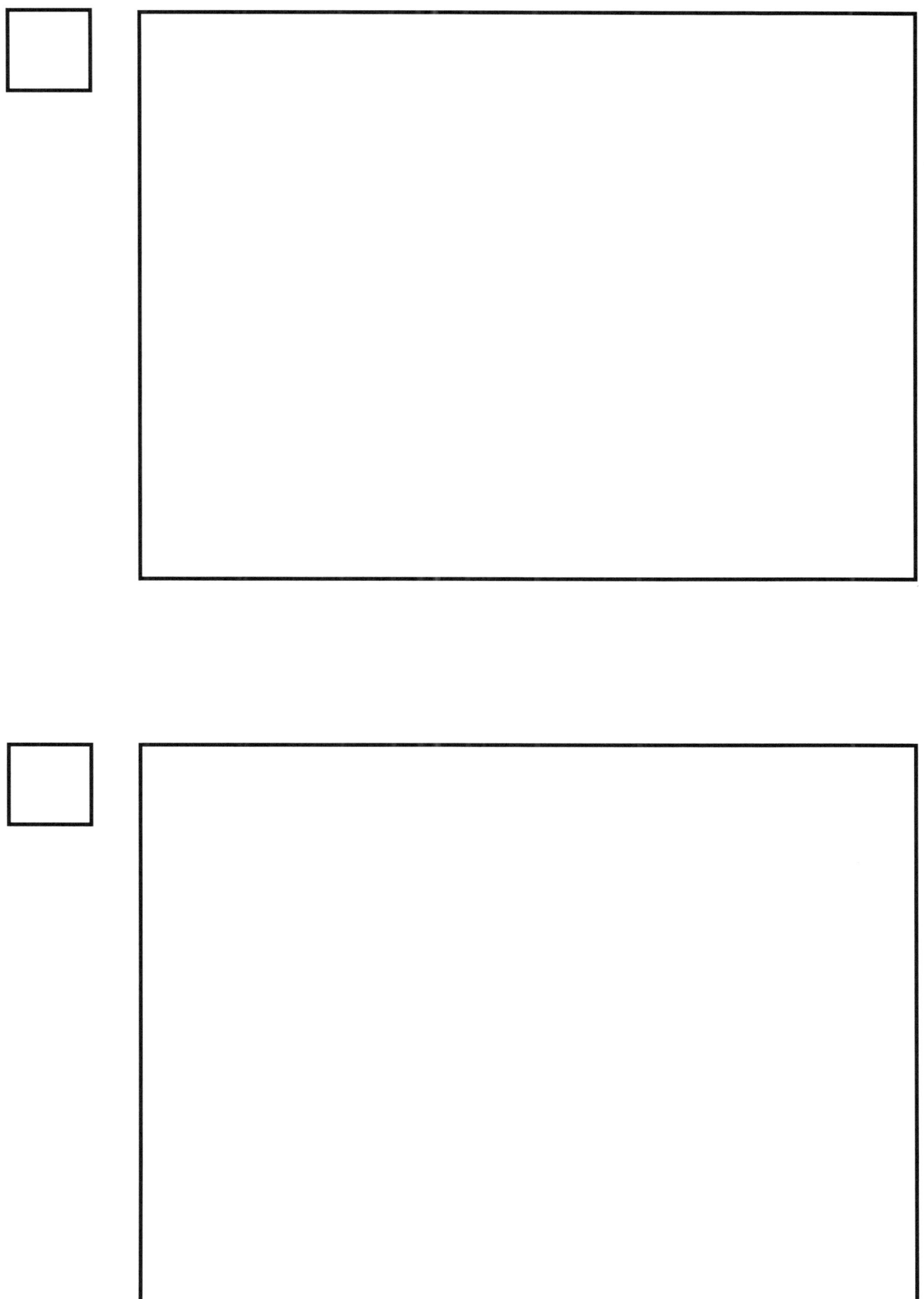

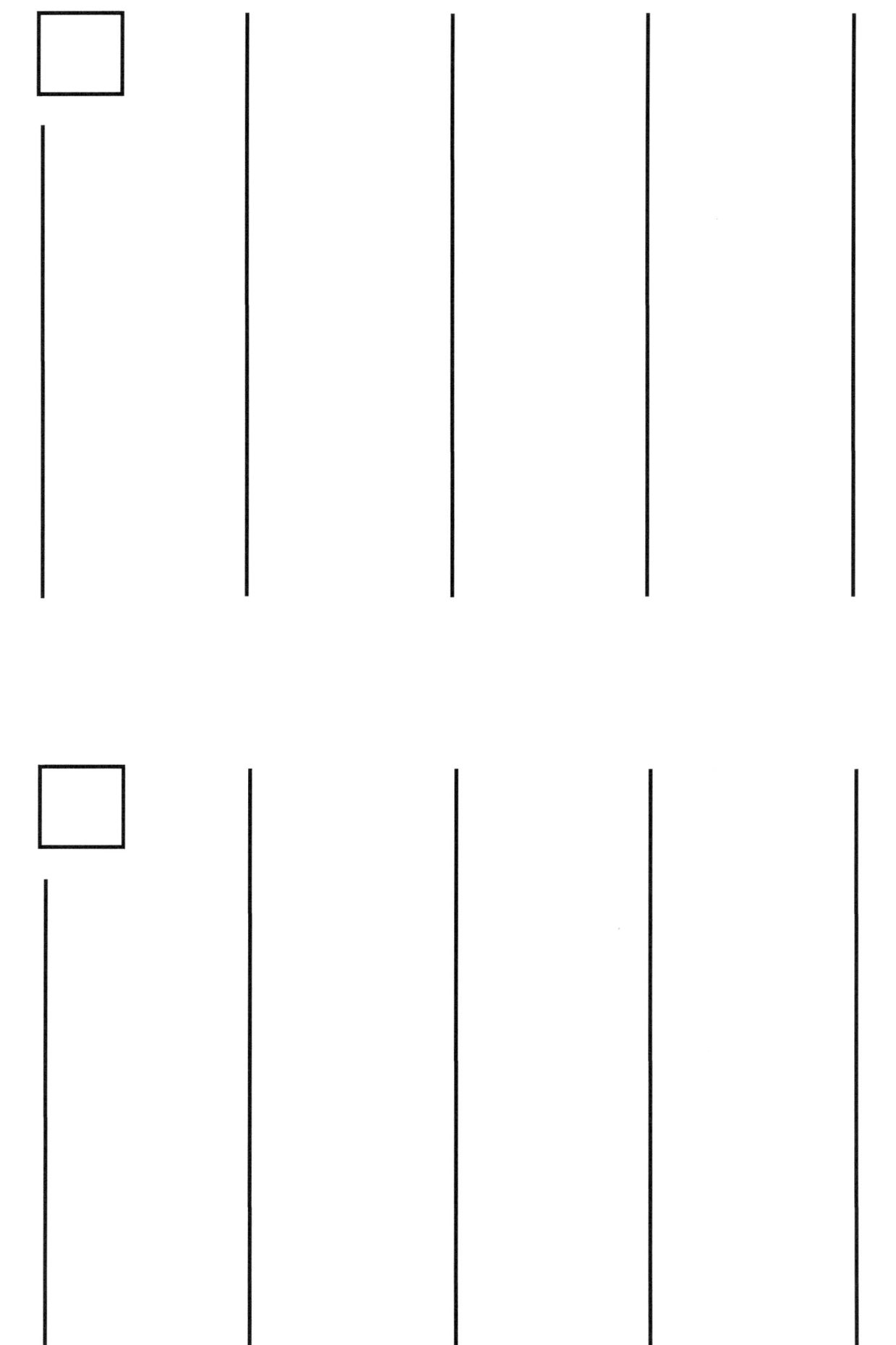

☐

References

☐

References

Author: _____   Peer Advisor: _____

Title ☐

Table of Contents ☐

Headings ☐

True Information About the Topic ☐

References ☐

Author: _____   Peer Advisor: _____

Title ☐

Table of Contents ☐

Headings ☐

True Information About the Topic ☐

References ☐

Title

Table of Contents

Headings

References

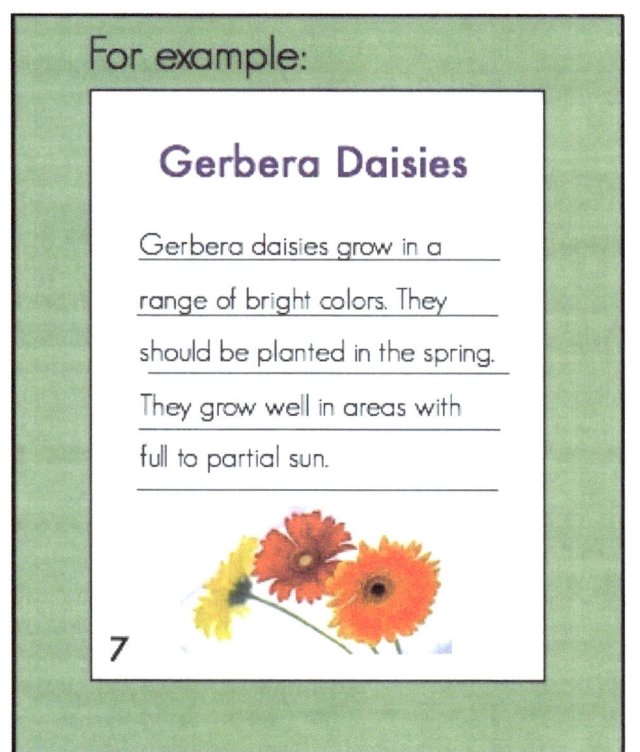

True Information About the Topic

1. Brainstorm a list of possible topics.

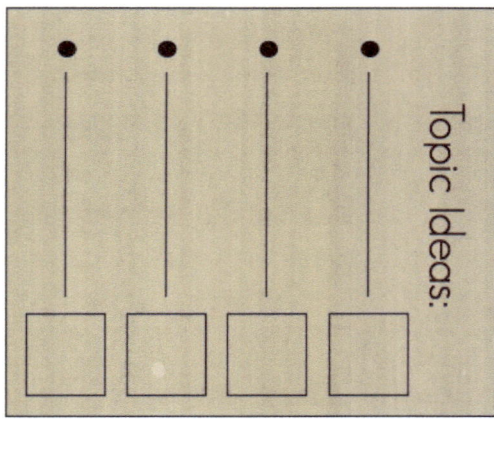

2. Choose one topic.

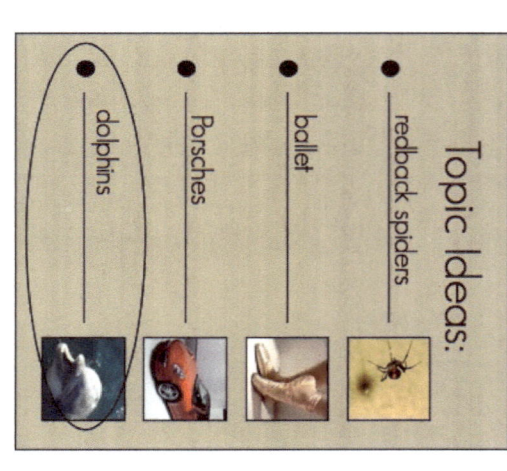

3. Research your topic.

4. Write the title.

5. Decide what your main categories will be. Write these in your table of contents.

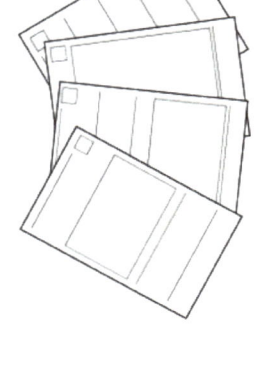

Table of Contents:
- Introduction
- Interesting Information
- Surprising Facts
- Frequently Asked Questions
- Further Reading
- About the Author
- References

6. Choose your paper. You might use the same type for every page, or a variety.

7. Write your first heading, which should match the first item in your table of contents. Use large print or color for the heading.

Introduction
This book is all about…

8. Write the words and draw or glue the pictures for this section. You may use one page, or more than one page, for the category.

For example:

Gerbera Daisies

Gerbera daisies grow in a range of bright colors. They should be planted in the spring. They grow well in areas with full to partial sun.

9. Repeat steps 7 and 8 for all of the categories in your table of contents.

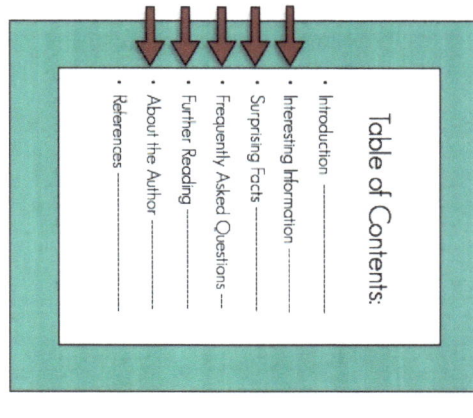

10. Write page numbers in the small box on each page in the book.

11. Write the appropriate page numbers on your table of contents page.

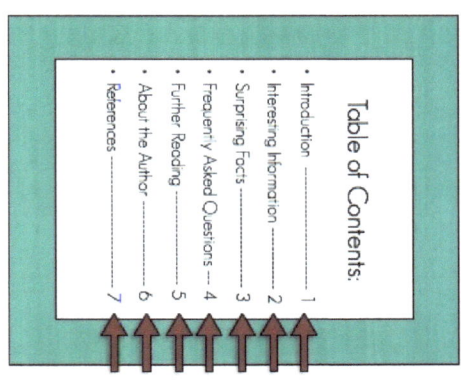

12. Write the names and information about your sources on the references page.

13. Revise using the checklist.

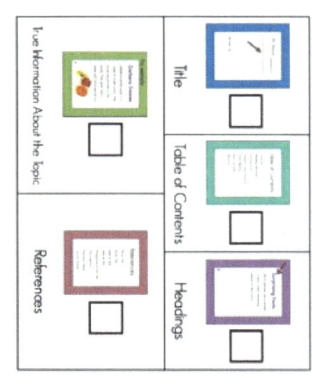

14. Start over at step 2.

Topic Ideas:
- redback spiders
- ballet
- Porsches
- dolphins

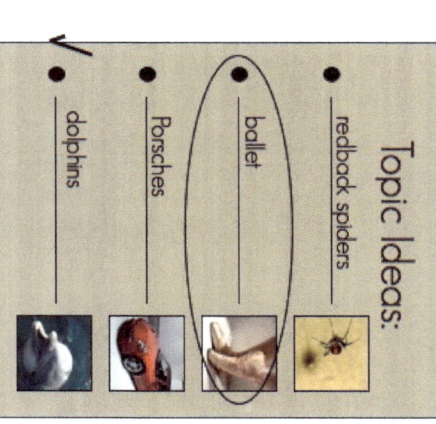

"You can tell people what you have been doing. I get ideas by really doing it! I get to use details and my imagination."

~ Ryan, age 6

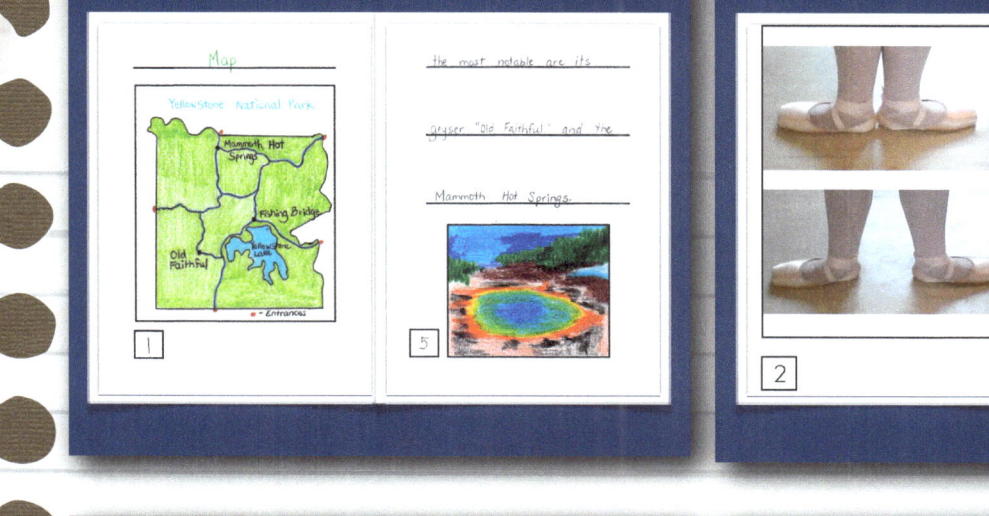
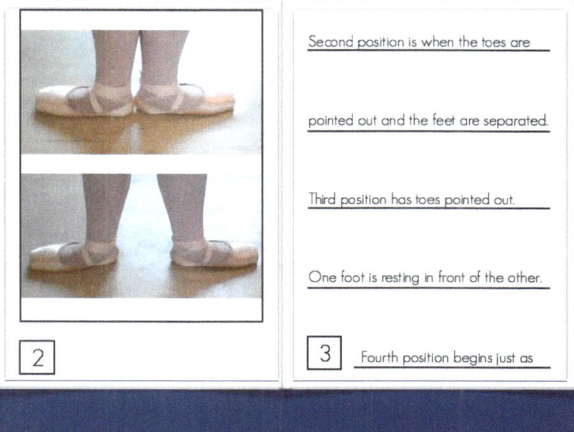
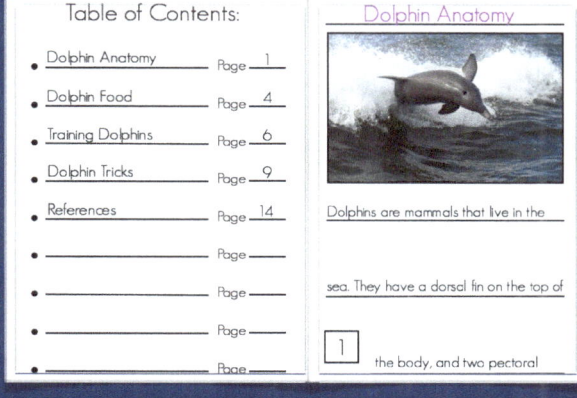

"ALL ABOUT" BOOKS MENTOR TEXTS

All About _____ Beagles

Title ☐	Table of Contents ☐
Headings ☐	
True Information About the Topic ☐	References ☐

Written By: _____

Date: _____

Table of Contents:

- Raising Beagle Puppies — Page ___
- Beagle Food — Page ___
- Beagle Behavior — Page ___
- Where to Get A Beagle — Page ___
- References — Page ___
- _____ — Page ___
- _____ — Page ___
- _____ — Page ___
- _____ — Page ___

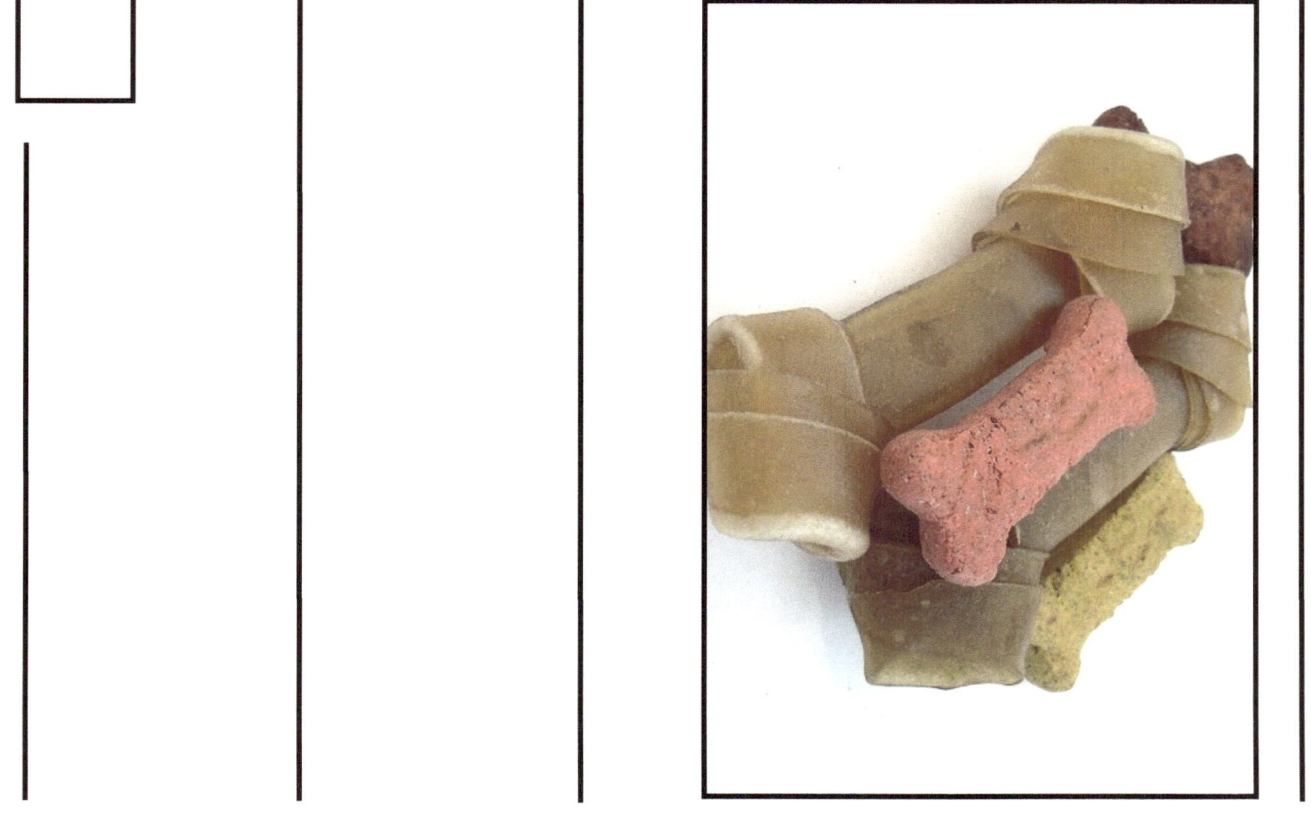

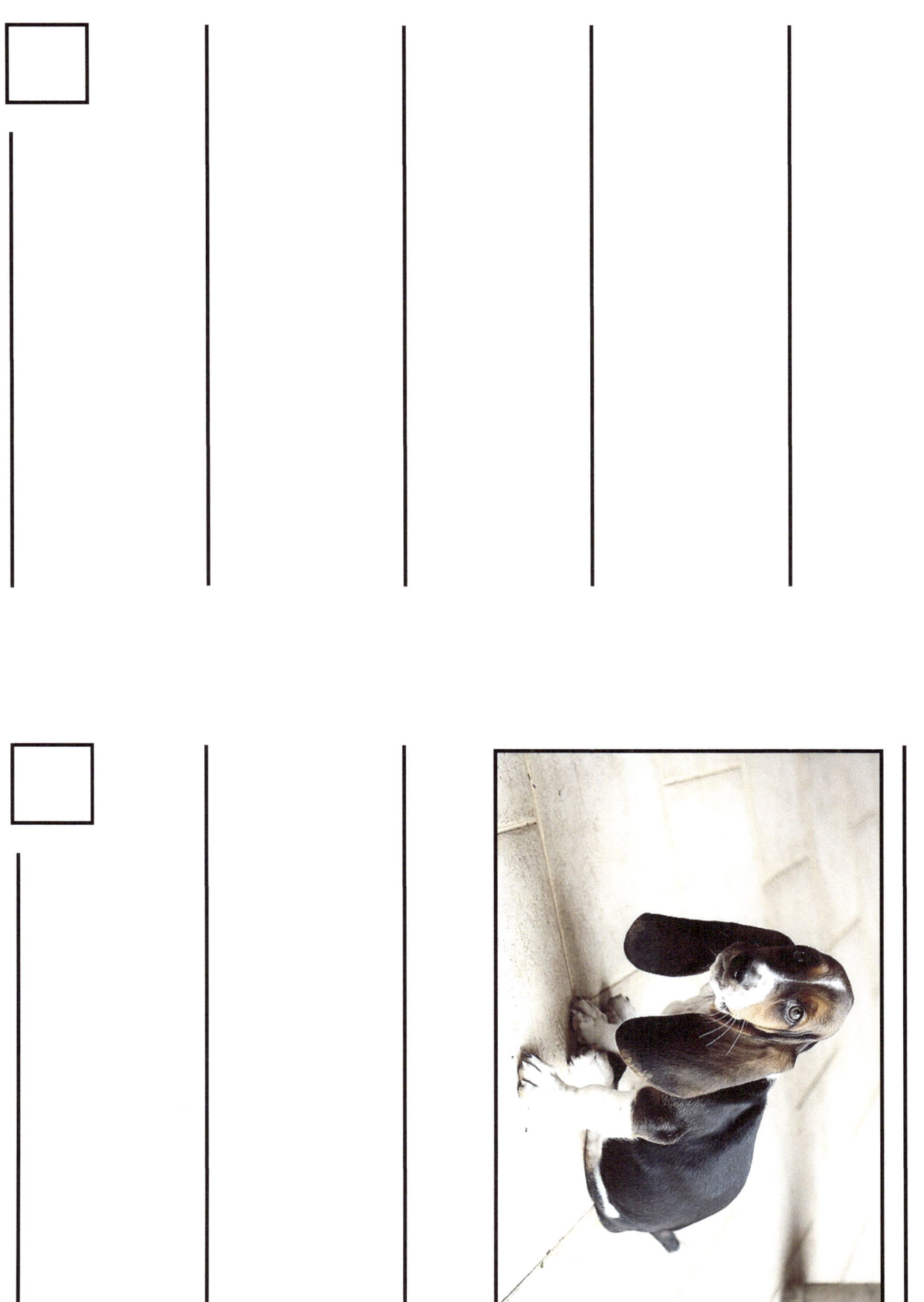

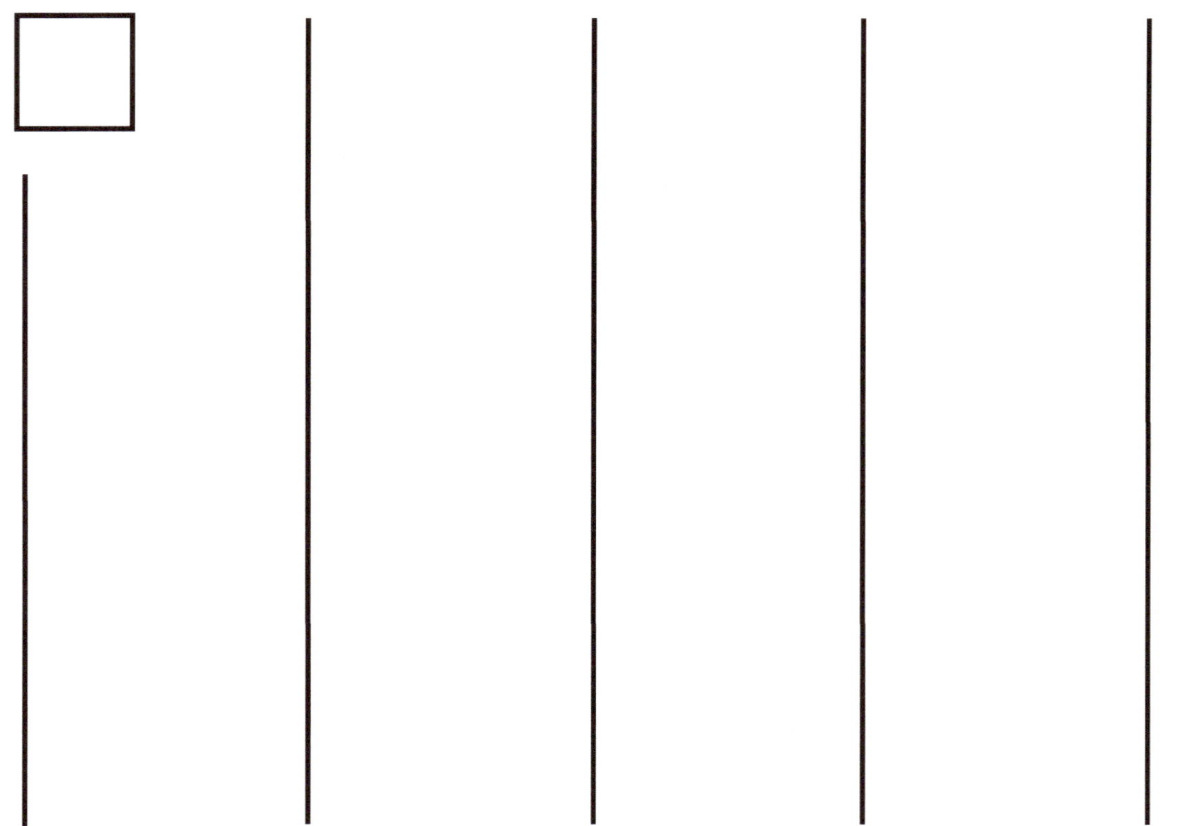

References

All About _____
Beagles

Title	Table of Contents	Headings

True Information About the Topic	References

Written By: _____ Karen Langdon

Date: _____ 8/12/16

Table of Contents:

- Raising Beagle Puppies .... Page 1
- Beagle Food .... Page 4
- Beagle Behavior .... Page 6
- Where to Get A Beagle .... Page 8
- References .... Page 10
- _____ .... Page ____
- _____ .... Page ____
- _____ .... Page ____
- _____ .... Page ____

Raising Beagle Puppies

Beagle puppies require patient, firm training. They also need to have regular

exercise to help them remain calm. Playing tracking games and purchasing animal scents will help satisfy the beagle puppy's hunting instinct.

The average size of a litter of beagle puppies is seven, with a range of two to

3
———————
fourteen.

Beagle Food

Beagle puppies require their mother's milk until they are eight weeks old. Solid

4
———————
food can be introduced at four

Beagle Behavior

Beagles are popular hunting dogs. They have a cheerful personality as well.

| 6 | They are social dogs that like to |

weeks of age. Beagles need a diet of 35-40% meat, 25-35% vegetables, and some starch. Pasta is a healthy option for a beagle.

| 5 |

be around people and other dogs. Beagles are easygoing and playful dogs. They are curious and fun loving!

7

Where to Get A Beagle

8

If you want a purebred beagle, you might need to purchase your dog through a breeder. There are many dogs available in animal shelters as well. You might just find a beagle!

9

References

- http://www.beaglepro.com/Feeding.html
- http://www.dogbreedinfo.com/beagle.htm
- http://www.woofipedia.com/discover/breeds/beagle
- https://www.akc.org/breeds/beagle/index.cfm

10

All About ____Ballet____

Title	Table of Contents
True Information About the Topic	Headings
	References

Written By: ____Karen Langdon____

Date: ____3/20/19____

Table of Contents:

- Basic Positions _____ Page __1__
- Ballet Shoes _____ Page __7__
- Learning to Dance Ballet _____ Page __9__
- Ballet in Art _____ Page __11__
- Famous Ballet Dancers _____ Page __14__
- References _____ Page __16__
- _____ Page ____
- _____ Page ____
- _____ Page ____

Basic Positions

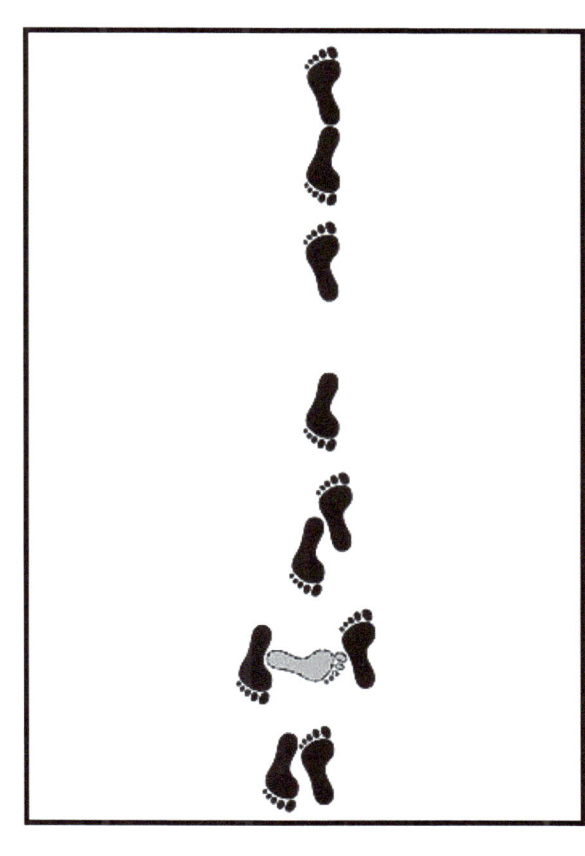

There are five basic positions in ballet.

First position is with the heels together

1 _____ and both toes pointed out.

2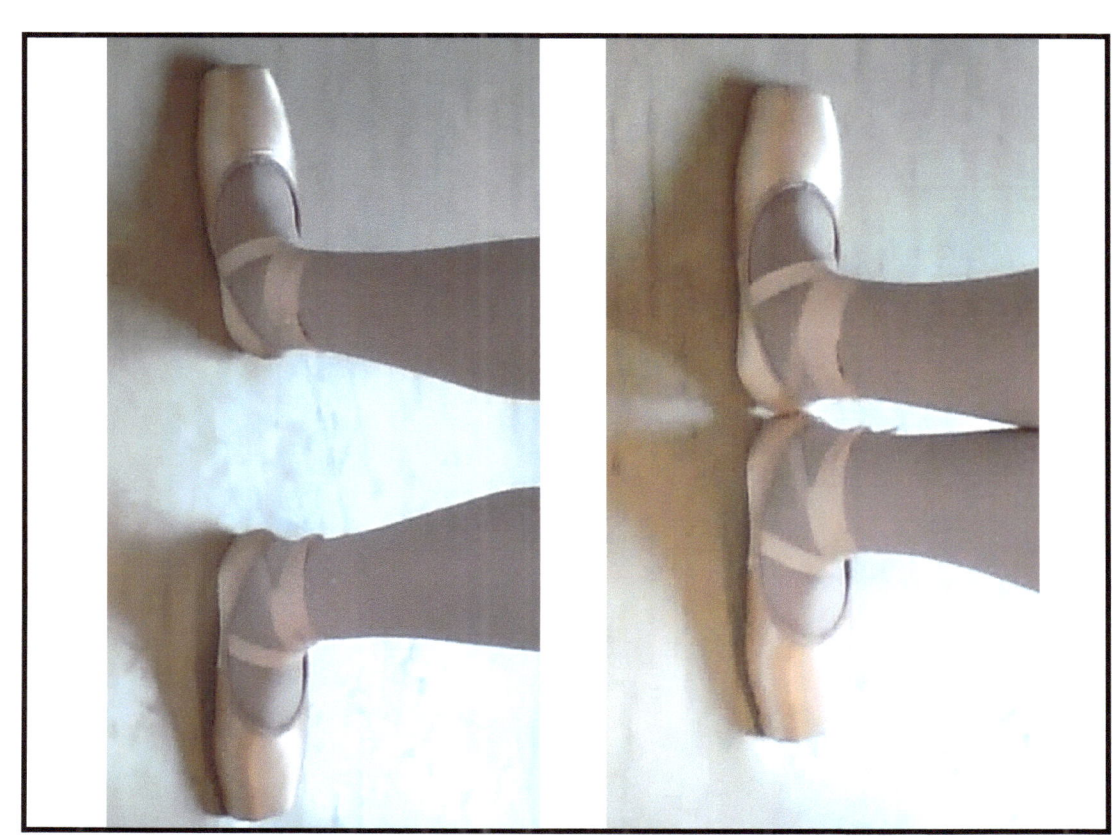

Second position is when the toes are pointed out and the feet are separated.

Third position has toes pointed out. One foot is resting in front of the other.

3

Fourth position begins just as third position, but one foot is about a foot's distance in front of the other.

Finally, fifth position is formed by having

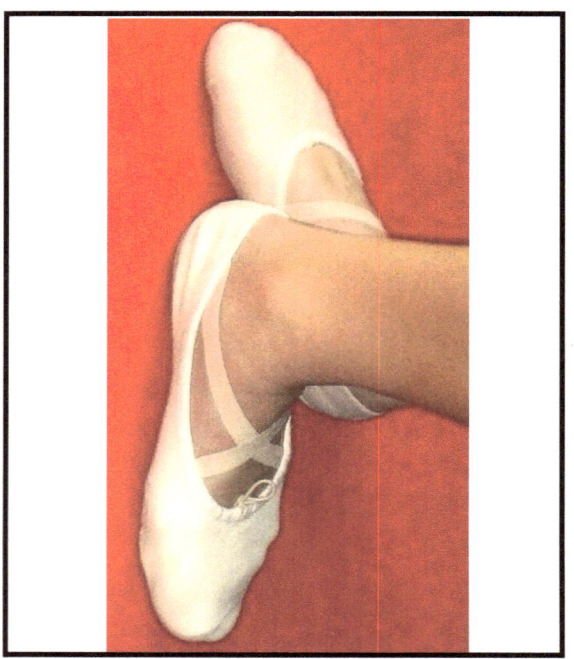

4

5 _____ _____ _____ _____ both feet back to back, with the toes pointing outwards in opposite directions.

6 _____

Ballet Shoes

There are two basic types of ballet

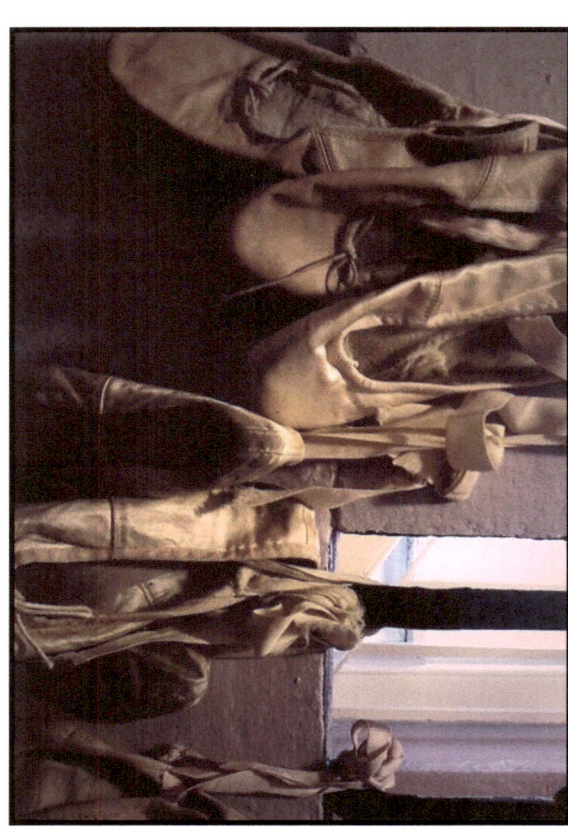

shoes. Ballet slippers are flexible and thin. Pointe shoes have a small block of cardboard near the toe. This supports the dancer as they stand on their toes.

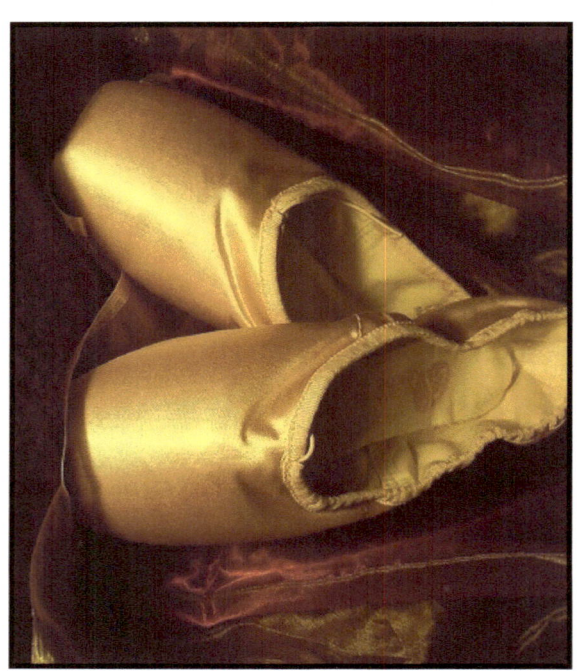

Learning to Dance Ballet

Many ballet dancers begin lessons at a very young age. Lessons teach students balance, grace, and poise. Even professional dancers continue to take lessons to practice their art.

Ballet in Art

Dance has inspired many artists. Edgar Degas is famous for painting approximately 1500 ballet scenes.

Famous Ballet Dancers

He painted dancers from unusual angles to show how the human body can move. Degas began sculpting later in his life, and he sculpted "The Little

| 13 | Dancer of Fourteen Years" in 1881.

Mikhail Baryshnikov is known as one of

| 14 | the greatest dancers of all time.

Anna Pavlova was the first prima ballerina to tour the world. She was an influential and charming dancer.

References

- http://www.danceclass.com/ballet-positions.html
- http://dance.about.com/od/youngdancers/p/Child_Dance.htm
- http://en.wikipedia.org/wiki/Ballet_shoe
- http://www.metmuseum.org/toah/hd/dgsp/hd_dgsp.htm
- http://www.telegraph.co.uk/culture/culturepicturegalleries/10663434/12-of-the-greatest-ballerinas-of-all-time.html
-
-

All About ___Chocolate___

Title	Table of Contents
	Headings
True Information About the Topic	References

Written By: ___Karen Langdon___

Date: ___10/12/14___

Table of Contents:

- Where Chocolate Comes From — Page 1
- Types of Chocolate — Page 4
- Fancy Chocolate — Page 6
- Chocolate and Fruit — Page 9
- References — Page 11
- — Page ___
- — Page ___
- — Page ___
- — Page ___
- — Page ___

Where Chocolate Comes From

Chocolate comes from the cacao tree. Pods filled <u>with seeds hang from</u>  these trees. When the seeds are dried they can

<u>be made into</u> 2

cocoa powder, and eventually chocolate. The first chocolate was made by the Mayans in Central America.

3

Types of Chocolate

There are many types of chocolate. The type of chocolate depends

4

on how the chocolate is prepared. Three common and popular types of chocolate are

5 dark, milk, and white.

6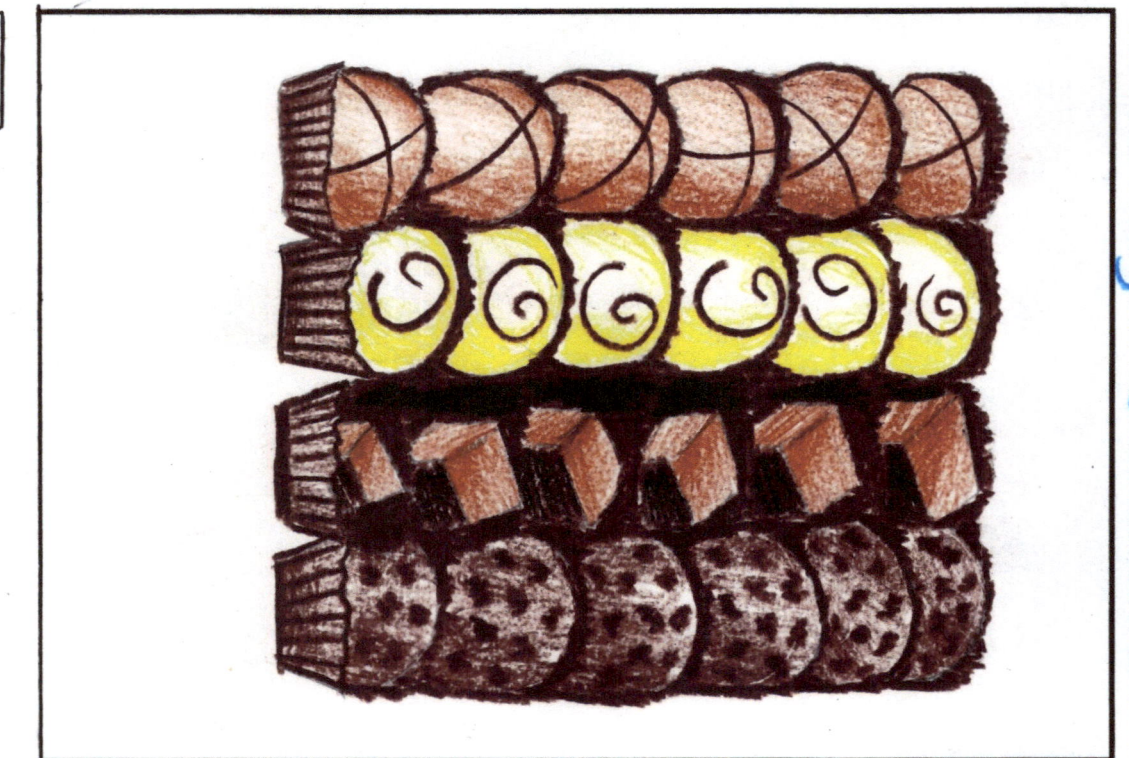

Fancy Chocolate

Chocolate is often decorated or made into fancy shapes. You can find chocolate sampler fancy chocolates. Chocolate can even be melted and made into a chocolate fountain!

7 boxes filled with

8 ___

Chocolate and Fruit

Chocolate is often paired with fruit. People enjoy chocolate covered strawberries, chocolate oranges, and even cherry filled chocolates.

9

10

References

- The Great Book of Chocolate
- David Lebovitz
- www.cadbury.com

All About ___Dolphins___

Title	Table of Contents	Headings

True Information About the Topic | References

Written By: ___Karen Langdon___

Date: ___9/10/15___

Table of Contents:

- Dolphin Anatomy .... Page __1__
- Dolphin Food .... Page __4__
- Training Dolphins .... Page __6__
- Dolphin Tricks .... Page __9__
- References .... Page __14__
- _____ Page ____
- _____ Page ____
- _____ Page ____

Dolphin Anatomy

Dolphins are mammals that live in the sea. They have a dorsal fin on the top of

1 the body, and two pectoral

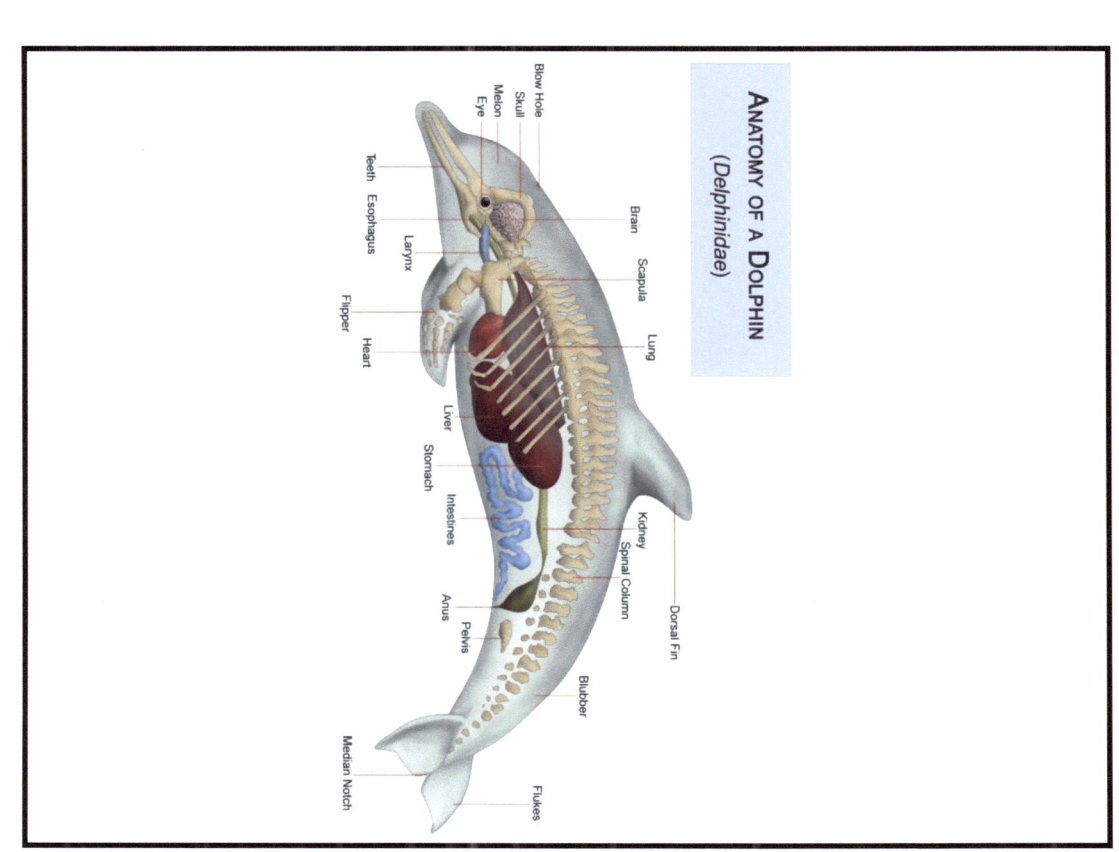

2

Dolphin Food

Wild dolphins catch their food and eat it under water. Dolphins eat fish, squid, and crustaceans. Each species ____4____

fins on the sides of the body. Dolphins have a blowhole on the top of their head, and they must come to the surface for air. There are 42 different ____3____ dolphin species in the world.

Training Dolphins

Training dolphins requires two way

communication between the

of dolphin eats a specific type of food.

An average size dolphin eats between 10 and 25 Kg of fish each day.

5 _____

6 _____

7

8

dolphin and the trainer. The trainer builds a friendship with the dolphin, and offers the dolphins rewards for specific behaviors. They use whistles and a training pole to communicate.

Dolphins Tricks

Dolphins can be trained to perform all sorts of tricks. They might be trained to

9

play with a ball or balance it

10

on their nose! They do jumps, flips, and receive praise and rewards (fish).

turns in the air, and some trainers even Dolphin shows are very popular, but

are able to stand and ride on a dolphin there are many groups fighting to stop

while it swims. Each time a dolphin

11 _____ performs a desired trick they

12 _____

them. They argue that dolphins belong in the ocean, and should not be entertainers. Many aquariums are now having education only dolphin shows.

13

References

- Everything Dolphins, Elizabeth Carney
- http://www.aqua.org
- http://www.dolphins-world.com
-

14

All About ___Yellowstone___
            ___National Park___

Title

Table of Contents

Headings

True Information About the Topic

References

Written By: __Karen Langdon__

Date: __9/2/15__

Table of Contents:

- Map ————————————— Page __1__
- History ————————————— Page __2__
- Geothermal Features ——————— Page __4__
- Wildlife ————————————— Page __6__
- References ———————————— Page __8__
- ——————————————————— Page ___
- ——————————————————— Page ___
- ——————————————————— Page ___
- ——————————————————— Page ___

Map

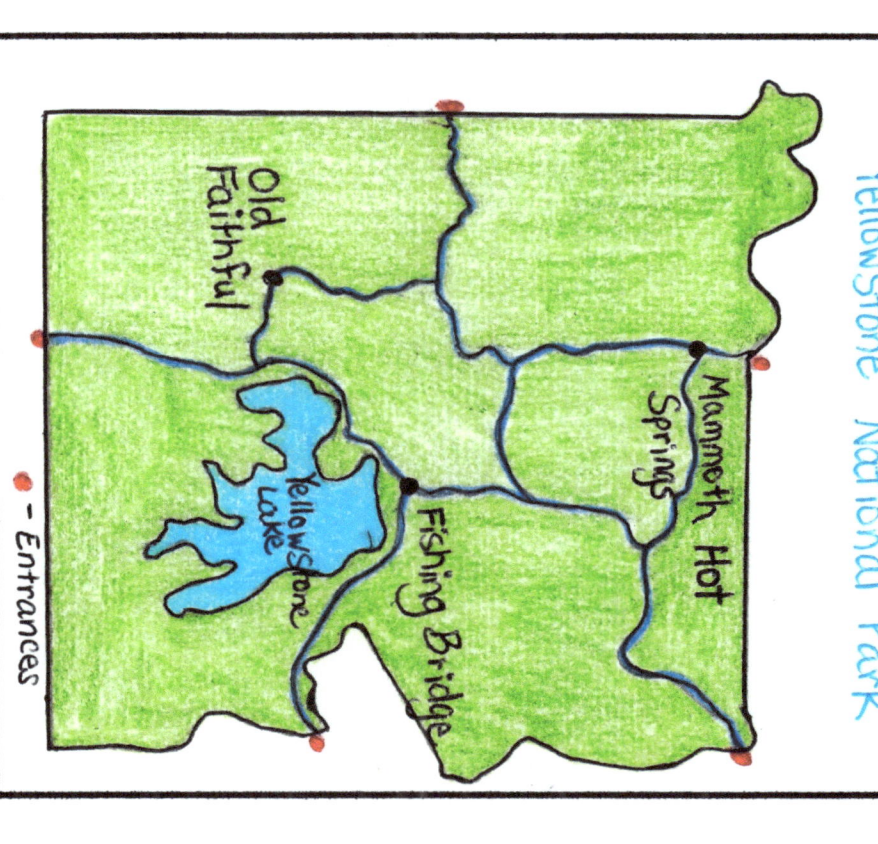

Yellowstone National Park

Old Faithful
Mammoth Hot Springs
Yellowstone Lake
Fishing Bridge
• - Entrances

1

History

Yellowstone National Park was established in 1872. Not only was it the first

2

national park in the

United States, but it was the first national park in the world.

3

Geothermal Features

Yellowstone National Park is home to a collection of geysers and hot springs. Two of

4

the most notable are its

geyser "Old Faithful" and the

Mammoth Hot Springs.

5

Wildlife

Wildlife viewing is popular at

6

Yellowstone. You can see

bison, elk, moose, and bears. There are also eagles, mountain goats, and pronghorn sheep.

7

References

- www.yellowstone-park.org
- www.nps.gov
- *The Yellowstone Park Foundation's Official Guide to Yellowstone National Park*, The Yellowstone Park Foundation
-

8

BEGINNING, MIDDLE & END MENTOR TEXTS

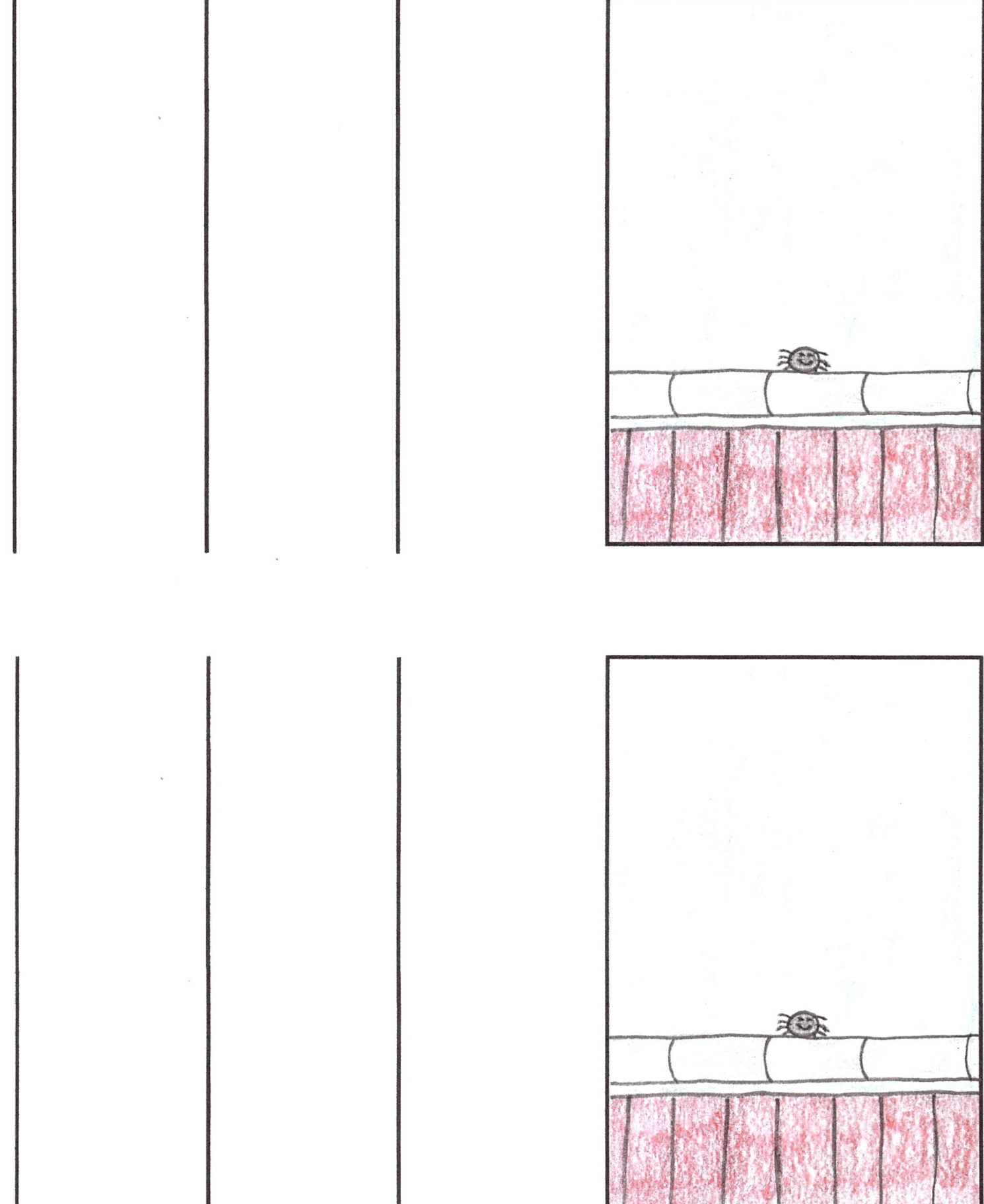

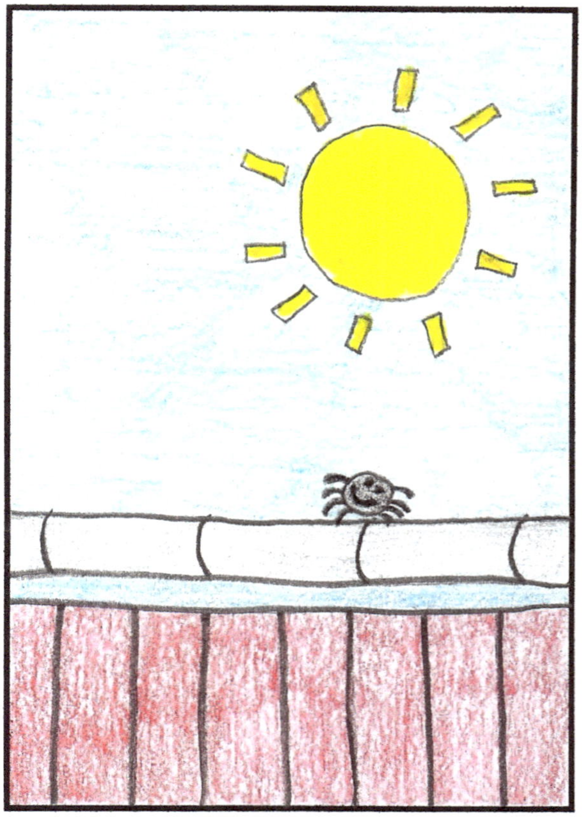

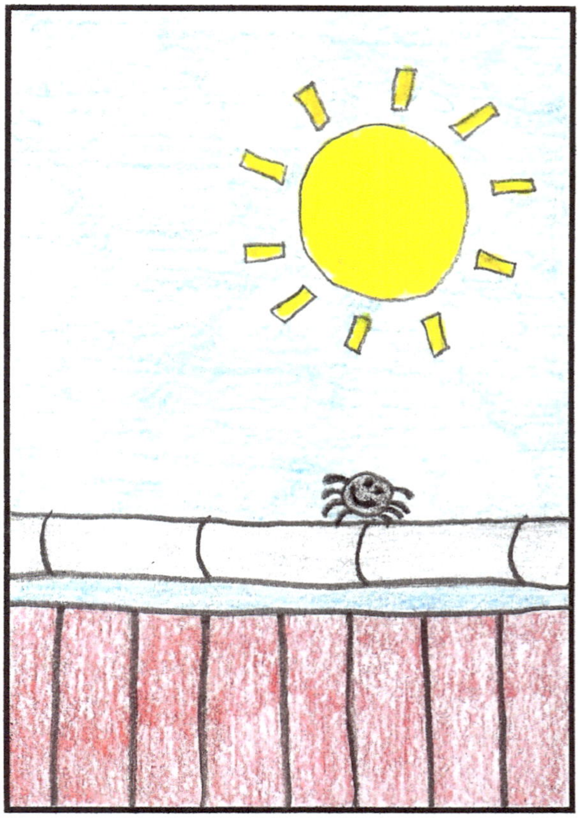

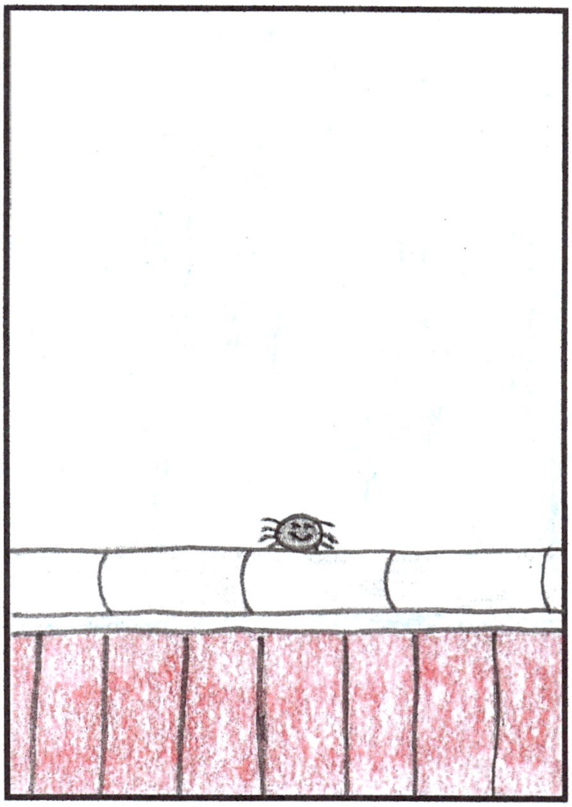

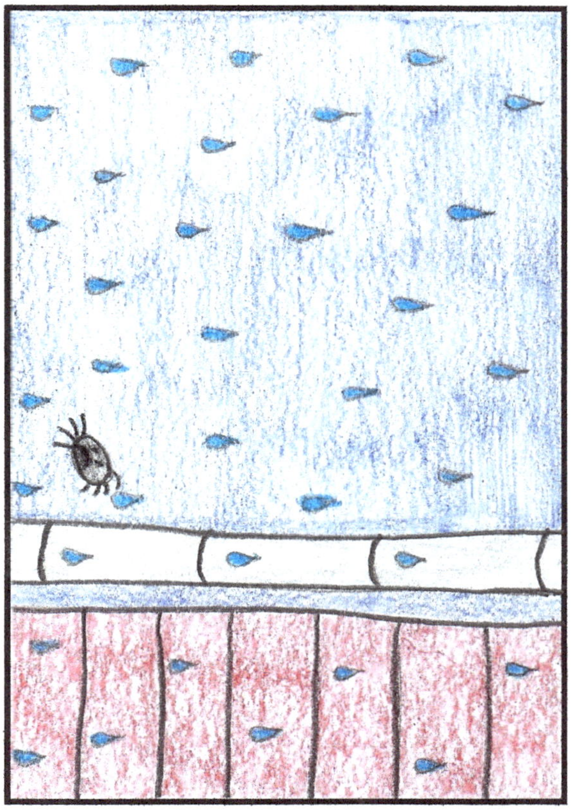

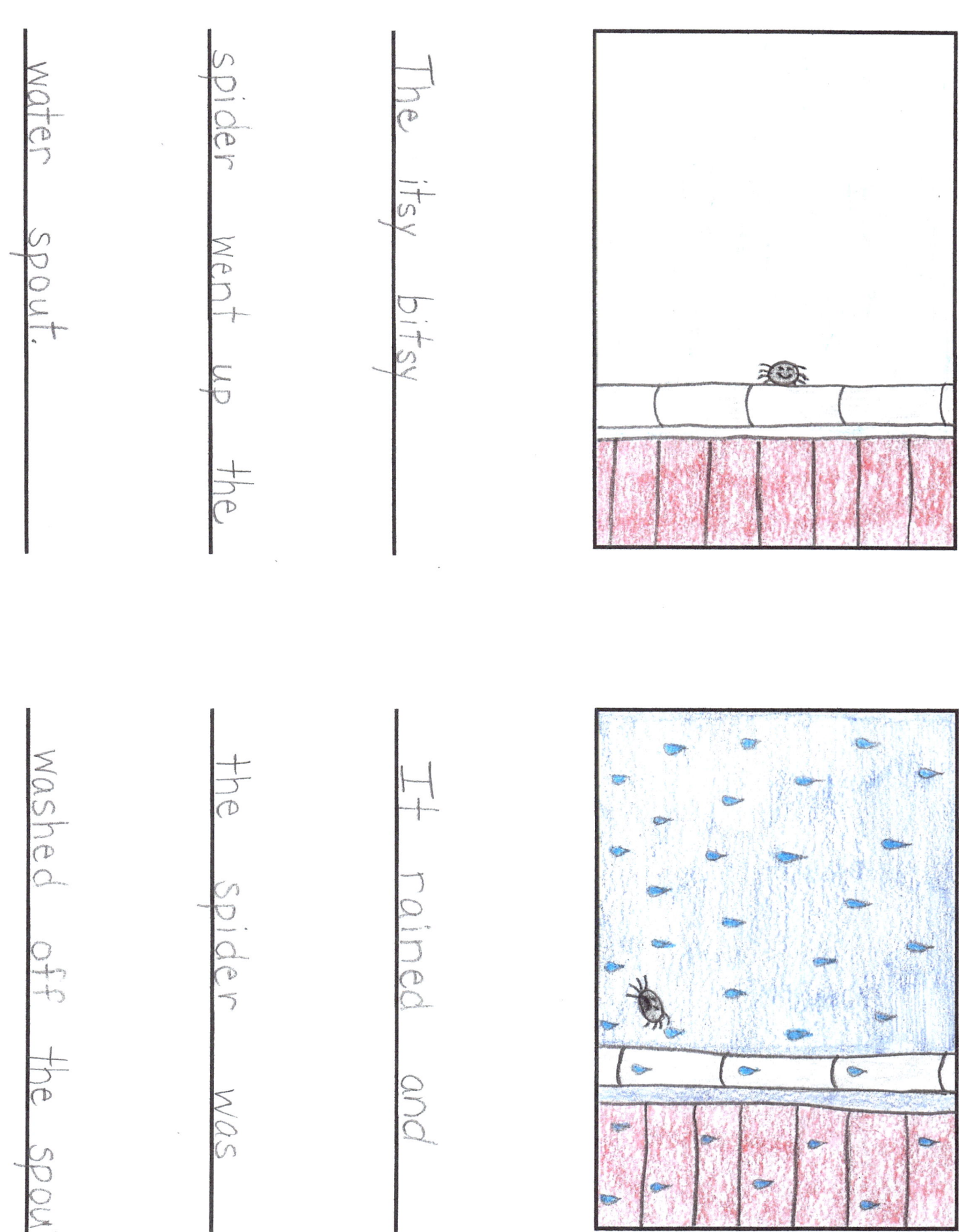

The itsy bitsy spider went up the water spout.

It rained and the spider was washed off the spout.

The sun dried everything and the spider climbed back up.

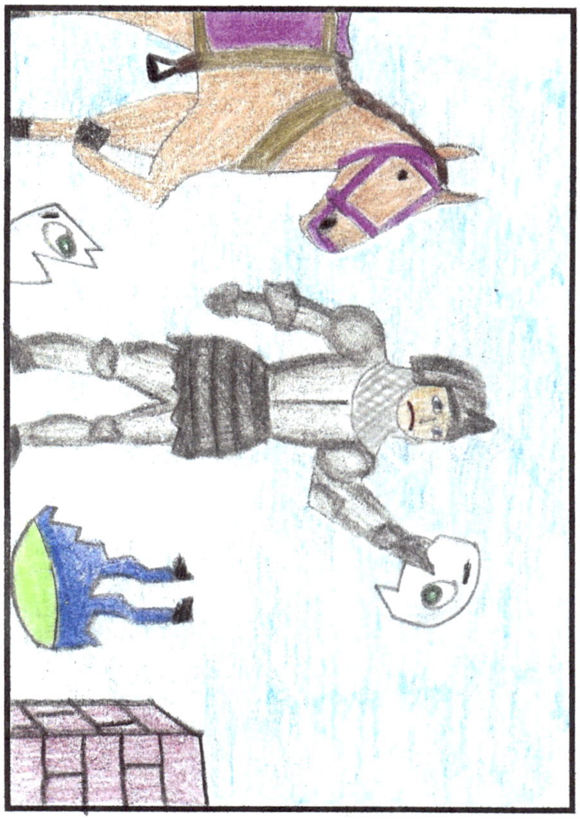

Humpty Dumpty
Sat on a wall.

He fell off of
the wall and
cracked.

All the king's horses

and men could not

fix Humpty Dumpty.

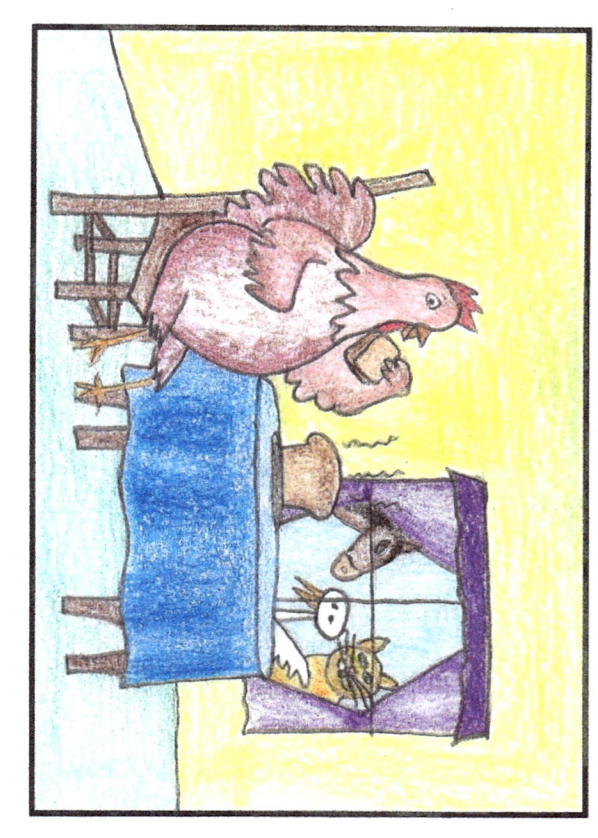

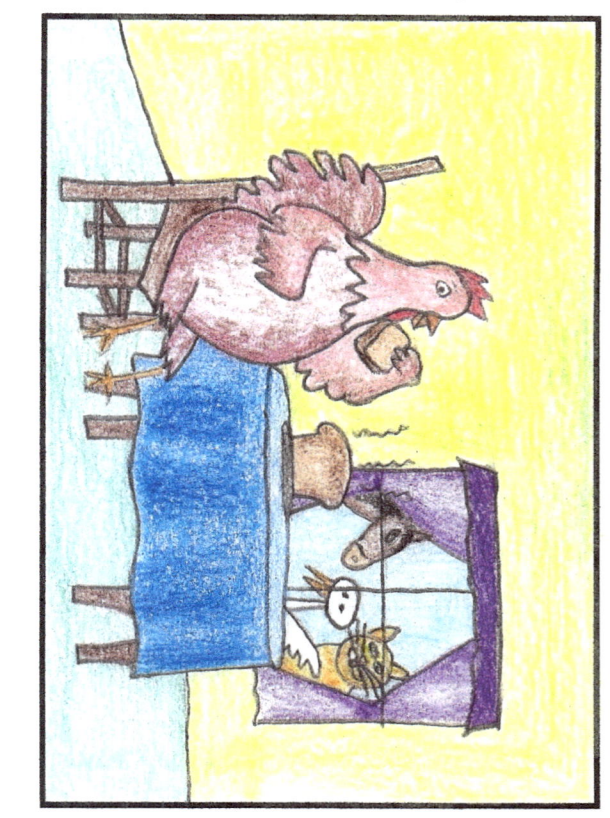

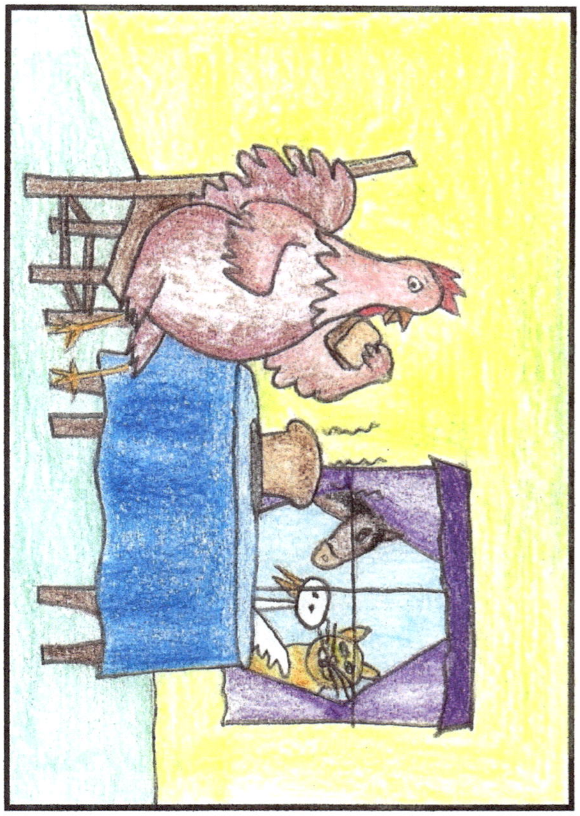

The little red hen
asked the animals
to help her.

All of the
animals were lazy
and would not help.

When the bread was done, the hen did not share with the animals.

The three little pigs built houses out of straw, sticks, and bricks.

The Big Bad Wolf came and tried to blow their houses down.

The wolf was frustrated because he could not blow the brick house down.

The wolf went down the chimney and landed in a pot of boiling water.

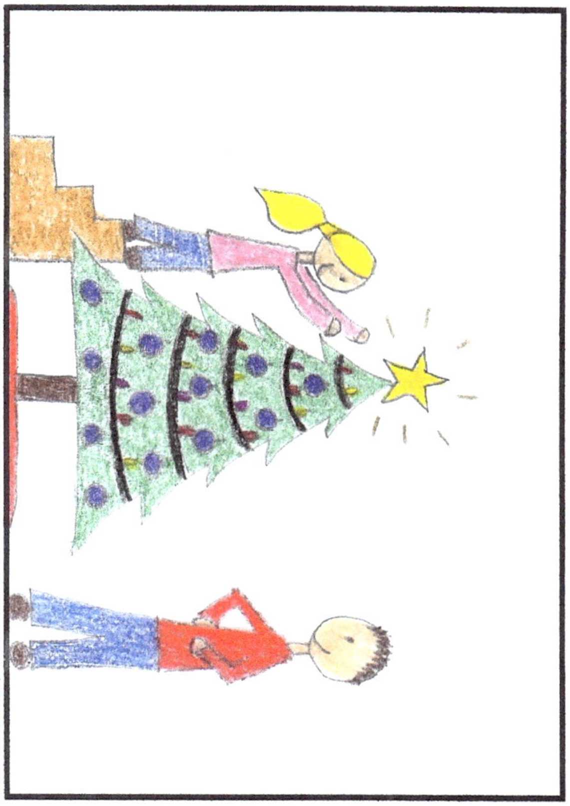

I helped my dad get our Christmas tree out of the box.

My dad strung lights on the tree while I hung ornaments.

Finally I got to put the star on top. I was so proud to finally be tall enough!

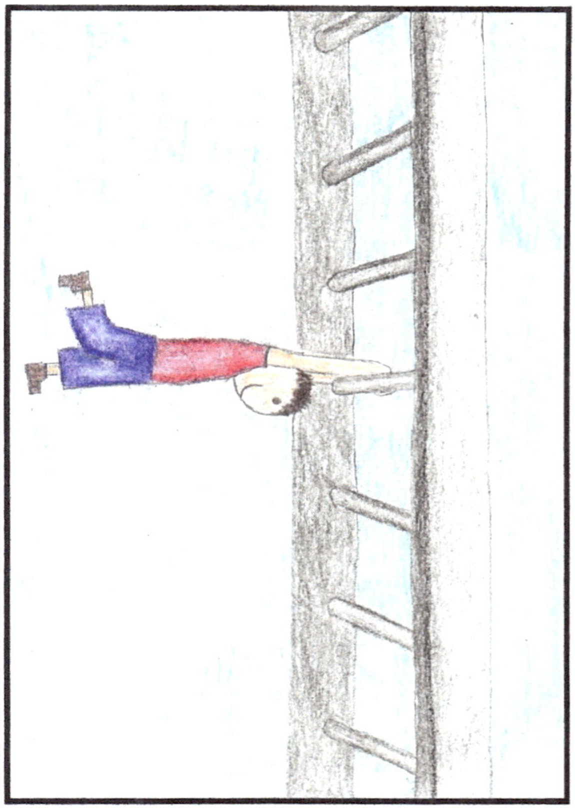

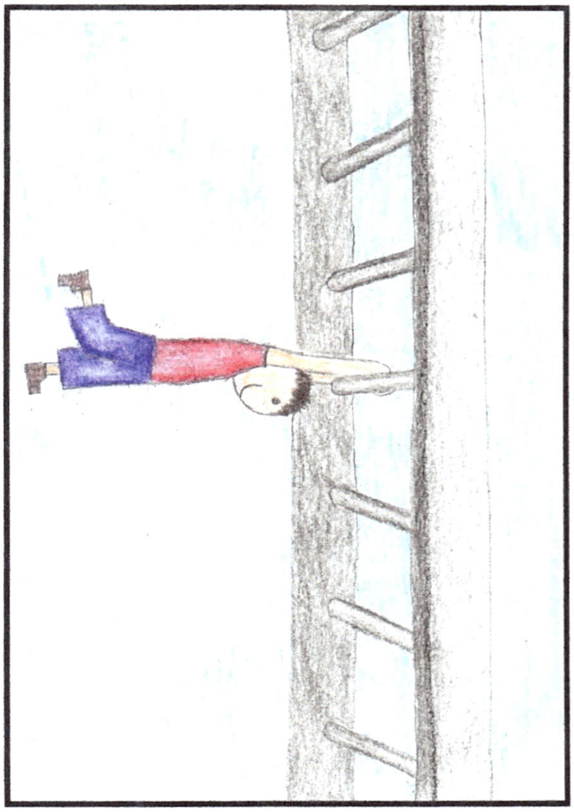

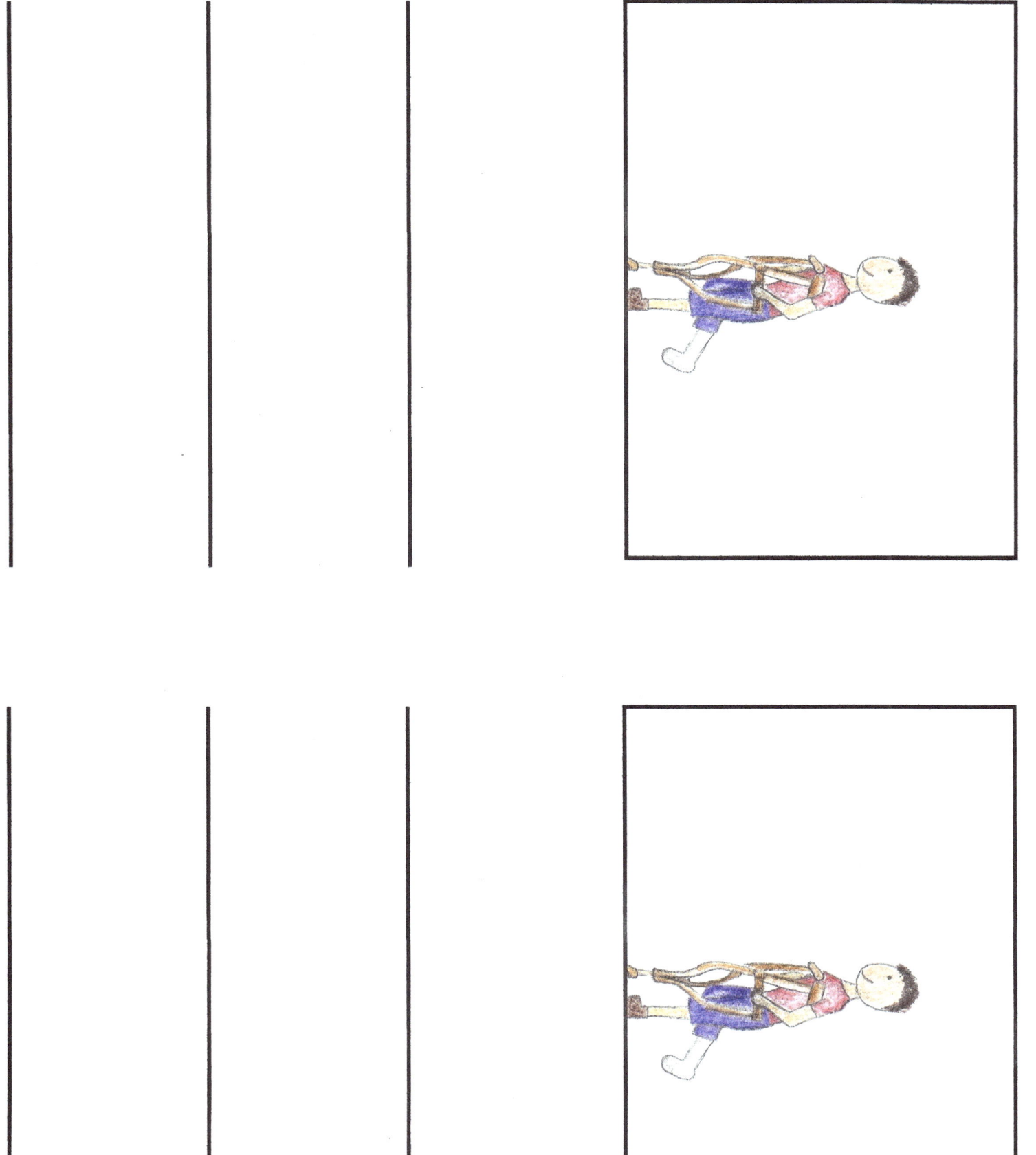

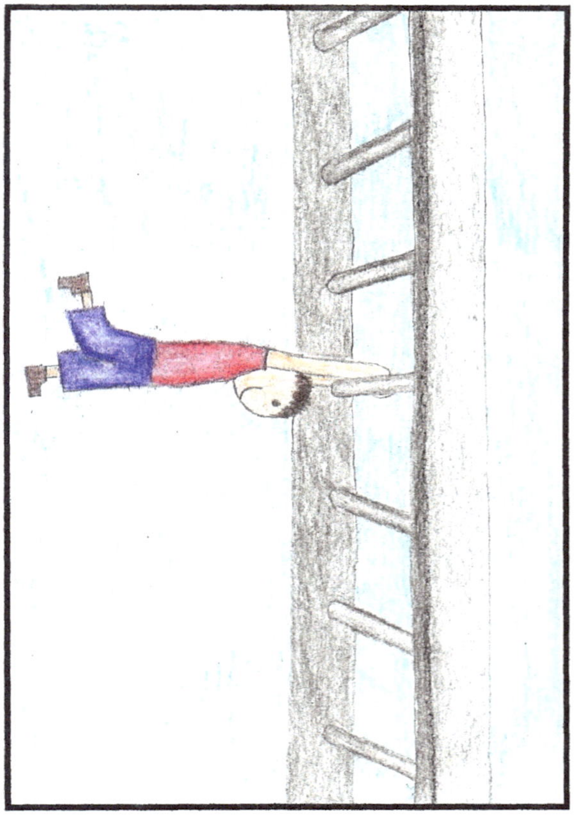

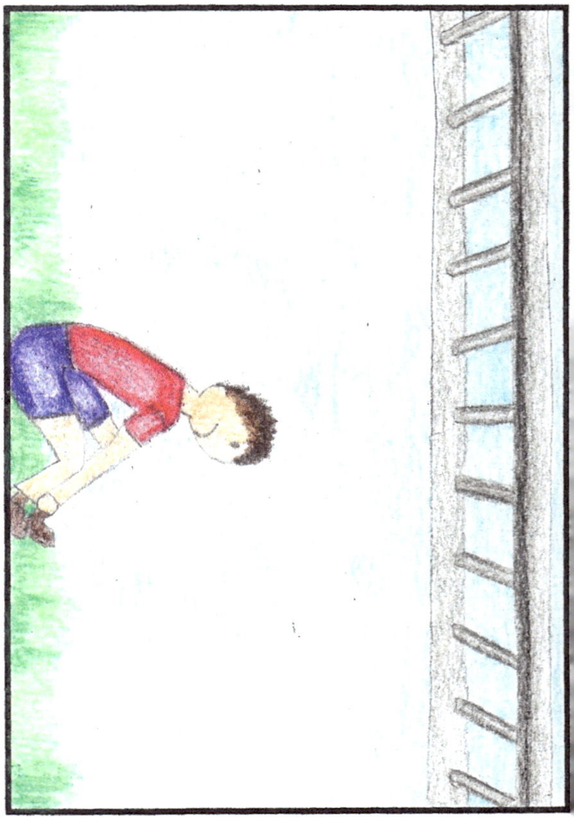

I was playing

on the monkey bars

at the park.

I slipped and fell!

I hurt my ankle. Tears

stung my eyes.

I had to go to the hospital and get a cast because my ankle was broken.

Now I am learning how to walk on crutches. I can't wait to get better!

"I really like writing because I can tell people about things I have done. I get my ideas by thinking back awhile ago about what happened. My favorite thing about writing is drawing the words."

~ Ben, age 6

Licensing Acknowledgements

I would like to thank all of the artists and photographers that so generously share their work for public use. The images used in this book were either my own photographs, or are acknowledged below. They are free to use via the creative commons for commercial use licensing.

The following images are protected under the Creative Commons 3.0 License, as reads: Attribution-ShareAlike 3.0 Unported (CC BY-SA 3.0)

animal shelter: http://commons.wikimedia.org/wiki/File:Quarantine_animal_shelter.JPG

beagle pup: http://commons.wikimedia.org/wiki/File:Beaglepuppysittingongrass.jpg

dolphin with one trainer: http://commons.wikimedia.org/wiki/File:Dolphin_and_trainer_4.jpg#file

dolphin anatomy: http://en.wikipedia.org/wiki/Dolphin#mediaviewer/File:Dolphin_anatomy.png

The following images belong to the Public Domain under the Creative Commons Public Domain Dedication, as reads:
CC0 1.0 Universal (CC0 1.0) Public Domain Dedication

ballet: http://pixabay.com/en/dance-ballet-dancers-271108/

girl on computer: http://pixabay.com/en/browsing-computer-female-floor-15824/

boy reading: http://pixabay.com/en/read-book-boy-child-kid-student-316507/

beagle pup 2: http://commons.wikimedia.org/wiki/File:Queen_Elizabeth_Pocket_Beagle_puppy.jpg

bone: http://pixabay.com/en/dog-bones-puppy-pet-dog-food-food-350094/

child ballerina: http://pixabay.com/en/ballet-dancers-backstage-stage-71002/

red check mark: http://pixabay.com/en/check-check-mark-red-mark-tick-303494/

back cover: http://pixabay.com/en/pencil-notebook-writing-notes-17808/

The following images are protected under the Creative Commons 2.0 License, as reads: Attribution-ShareAlike 2.0 Generic (CC BY-SA 2.0)

child writing: http://commons.wikimedia.org/wiki/File:A-kid-drawing-or-writing.jpg
two hands writing: http://www.flickr.com/photos/25596604@N04/3427826247
redback spider: https://www.flickr.com/photos/wikiwill/3564235479/
dolphin close up: http://de.fotopedia.com/items/flickr-98391847
Porsche: http://commons.wikimedia.org/wiki/File:2012_NAIAS_Red_Porsche_991_convertible_(world_premiere).jpg
gerbera daisy: https://www.flickr.com/photos/vironevaeh/4920724594/
beagle 1: https://www.flickr.com/photos/and1/2615231317/
beagle running: https://www.flickr.com/photos/24917549@N04/3501213599/
pencils: http://www.flickr.com/photos/21093323@N02/2376598010
who/what: http://www.flickr.com/photos/39151020@N03/4319112328
setting: http://www.flickr.com/photos/kevinsaff/3272619731
feeling: http://www.flickr.com/photos/8489692@N03/4334102263
feeling / five senses: http://www.flickr.com/photos/33904751@N04/5084847252
beginning, middle, end: http://www.flickr.com/photos/73344134@N00/2070268674
child writing: http://commons.wikimedia.org/wiki/File:A-kid-drawing-or-writing.jpg
dolphin blowhole: https://www.flickr.com/photos/fleur-design/458562940/
dolphin with ball: https://www.flickr.com/photos/hamed/123715681/
dolphin training group: https://www.flickr.com/photos/rosshawkes/5549926648/
Degas statue: https://www.flickr.com/photos/photogaby/2942311597/
ballet shoes: https://www.flickr.com/photos/craiglea/3241156189/
toe shoes: https://www.flickr.com/photos/megyarsh/2305528652/
ballet class: https://www.flickr.com/photos/jbach/745967636/
roasting marshmallows - http://www.flickr.com/photos/94693506@N00/195879959
Lego - http://www.flickr.com/photos/oskay/2157692222/
marshmallows - http://www.flickr.com/photos/8489692@N03/5000710747
stick - http://www.flickr.com/photos/71861129@N00/241466851
skewer - http://www.flickr.com/photos/22809317@N04/3053571051
friends - http://www.flickr.com/photos/38582236@N06/4498154383
pencils: http://www.flickr.com/photos/21093323@N02/2376598010

The following images were sourced from Wikipedia Commons, and are referenced according to their terms, as follows:

dolphin balancing trick: By Zamzavkaftyaf (Own work) [CC-BY-SA-3.0 (http://creativecommons.org/licenses/by-sa/3.0) or GFDL (http://www.gnu.org/copyleft/fdl.html)], via Wikimedia Commons

two jumping dolphins: By Anagoria (Own work) [GFDL (http://www.gnu.org/copyleft/fdl.html) or CC-BY-3.0 (http://creativecommons.org/licenses/by/3.0)], via Wikimedia Commons

dolphin eating: By frank wouters (Flickr) [CC-BY-2.0 (http://creativecommons.org/licenses/by/2.0)], via Wikimedia Commons

ballet blue jump: By Jeff from Denver, US (grace in winter 2 Uploaded by Ekabhishek) [CC-BY-SA-2.0 (http://creativecommons.org/licenses/by-sa/2.0)], via Wikimedia Commons

ballet point: By Loadmaster (David R. Tribble) This image was made by Loadmaster (David R. Tribble) Email the author: David R. Tribble Also see my personal gallery at Google Picasa (Own work) [CC-BY-SA-3.0 (http://creativecommons.org/licenses/by-sa/3.0) or GFDL (http://www.gnu.org/copyleft/fdl.html)], via Wikimedia Commons

1st: "Première pointes". Licensed under Creative Commons Attribution-Share Alike 3.0 via Wikimedia Commons - http://commons.wikimedia.org/wiki/File:Premi%C3%A8repointes.PNG#mediaviewer/File:Premi%C3%A8repointe.sPNG

2nd: http://commons.wikimedia.org/wiki/File:Secondepointes.PNG#file
positions: By User:Martiny (footprint image taken from File:Happy feet 2.svg) [Public domain], via Wikimedia Commons

3rd: By Iruka (Own work) [GFDL (http://www.gnu.org/copyleft/fdl.html), CC-BY-SA-3.0 (http://creativecommons.org/licenses/by-sa/3.0/) or CC-BY-SA-2.5-2.0-1.0 (http://creativecommons.org/licenses/by-sa/2.5-2.0-1.0)], via Wikimedia Commons

4th: "Quatrième demipointes". Licensed under Creative Commons Attribution-Share Alike 3.0 via Wikimedia Commons - http://commons.wikimedia.org/wiki/File:Quatri%C3%A8me_demipointes.PNG#mediaviewer/File:Quatri%C3%A8me_demipointes.PNG

4th man: By Fanny Schertzer (Own work) [GFDL (http://www.gnu.org/copyleft/fdl.html) or CC-BY-SA-3.0-2.5-2.0-1.0 (http://creativecommons.org/licenses/by-sa/3.0)], via Wikimedia Commons

Baryshnikov: By Knight Foundation (Flickr: YoungArts 2010) [CC-BY-SA-2.0 (http://creativecommons.org/licenses/by-sa/2.0)], via Wikimedia Commons

Anna Pavlova: http://en.wikipedia.org/wiki/Anna_Pavlova#mediaviewer/File:AP_Cygne.jpg
Degas: Edgar Degas [Public domain or Public domain], via Wikimedia Commons

black girl writing: By Erica Szlosek, U.S. Fish and Wildlife Service [Public domain], via Wikimedia Commons

The following images are protected under the Creative Commons 2.0 License, as reads: Attribution-NoDerivs 2.0 Generic (CC BY-ND 2.0)

    fish on a hook - http://www.flickr.com/photos/22869502@N04/3590382389
    French braid - http://www.flickr.com/photos/34176077@N02/5186799077
    camp fire - http://www.flickr.com/photos/8950560@N08/3830882258
    can of pens and pencils: http://www.flickr.com/photos/23995388@N02/3871984162

Usage rights for the following images were purchased from these sources:

- torn paper - © Sak12344 | Dreamstime.com - Single Page Torn From Notebook Photo
- girl writing - © Kolinkotanya | Dreamstime.com - Child Is Writing Photo
- girl writing 2 - © Andresr | Dreamstime.com - Little Girl Studying Photo
- girl writing 3 - © Kolinkotanya | Dreamstime.com - Girl Writing Photo
- boy writing - © Carline1 | Dreamstime.com - Early Learning Photo
- boy writing 2 - © Tatyanagl | Dreamstime.com - Kid Does Lessons Lying On The Floor Photo

Information that was included in the "All About" books mentor texts came from the following sources:

Beagle information:
- http://www.beaglepro.com/Feeding.html
- http://www.dogbreedinfo.com/beagle.htm
- http://www.woofipedia.com/discover/breeds/beagle
- https://www.akc.org/breeds/beagle/index.cfm

Dolphin information:
- Everything Dolphins, Elizabeth Carney
- http://www.aqua.org
- http://www.dolphins-world.com

Ballet information:
- http://www.telegraph.co.uk/culture/culturepicturegalleries/10663434/12-of-the-greatest-ballerinas-of-all-time.html
- http://en.wikipedia.org/wiki/Ballet_shoe
- http://dance.about.com/od/youngdancers/p/Child_Dance.htm
- http://www.danceclass.com/ballet-positions.html
- http://www.metmuseum.org/toah/hd/dgsp/hd_dgsp.htm

Yellowstone information:
- http://www.yellowstone-park.org
- http://www.nps.gov
- The Yellowstone Park Foundation's Official Guide to Yellowstone National Park, The National Park Foundation

Chocolate information:
- http://www.cadbury.com
- The Great Book of Chocolate, David Lebovitz

Contacts and Terms of Use

I am committed to providing teachers with relevant and useful instructional materials and activities that inspire creative and critical thinking while building authenticity in the classroom.

Follow Me!

http://www.teachingace.com
http://www.teacherspayteachers.com/Store/Karen-Langdon
https://www.facebook.com/TeachingAce
http://pinterest.com/karenelangdon
https://twitter.com/teachingace1
Instagram: teachingace1

By purchasing this item you are agreeing that the product is the property of Karen Langdon and is licensed to you to use for personal and classroom use only. Karen Langdon retains the copyright and reserves all rights to this product. You MAY: Use this product for your own personal use or classroom use. You MAY NOT: Claim this work as your own, sell this product to others, or share this product with others. Redistributing, editing, selling, or posting this item (or any part thereof) on the Internet are all strictly prohibited without first gaining permission from the author.

Copyright © 2014 Karen Langdon All rights reserved by author. Permission to copy for classroom use only.

www.ingramcontent.com/pod-product-compliance
Lightning Source LLC
Chambersburg PA
CBHW041151290426
44108CB00002B/32